GET OVER YOURSELF: LEARNING HOW TO MANAGE YOUR ANGER

A TRAINER'S MANUAL

DR. JOAN D. ATWOOD

**GET OVER YOURSELF: LEARNING HOW TO MANAGE YOUR ANGER
A TRAINER'S MANUAL**

iUniverse books may be ordered through booksellers or by contacting:

*iUniverse
1663 Liberty Drive
Bloomington, IN 47403
www.iuniverse.com
1-800-Authors (1-800-288-4677)*

*Because of the dynamic nature of the Internet, any web addresses or links contained in
this book may have changed since publication and may no longer be valid. The views
expressed in this work are solely those of the author and do not necessarily reflect the
views of the publisher, and the publisher hereby disclaims any responsibility for them.*

*Any people depicted in stock imagery provided by Getty Images are models,
and such images are being used for illustrative purposes only.
Certain stock imagery © Getty Images.*

*ISBN: 978-1-5320-9550-4 (sc)
ISBN: 978-1-5320-9552-8 (e)*

Print information available on the last page.

iUniverse rev. date: 03/11/2020

THE ANGER MANAGEMENT
PROFESSIONAL CERTIFICATION PROGRAM

TABLE OF CONTENTS

DETAILED TABLE OF CONTENTS

MODULE I

OVERVIEW OF THE PROGRAM

How To Use This Program

This course is separated into twelve modules. Each module provides the Professional with information about Anger Management. In addition, it provides the Professional with the materials necessary to run a 12 session group. All forms and exercises are included within the text on separate sheets that may be Xeroxed for participants to use.

The Program is progressive in that each module builds on the one prior. While each module stands alone, it is useful to follow the module order so that the probing and exploration into their anger response by the participant deepens as they progress.

This program teaches the professional the information necessary to see individual clients for Anger Management or to run groups. Please keep in mind that it is believed that a 12 session program is the tip of the iceberg. It by no means will "cure" a person of their anger response. It will help them gain control over it. It will help them become more aware of the triggering responses and how they define their triggering responses. The program is not appropriate for persons with deep seated psychological problems. It is appropriate for persons who truly wish to gain control over their anger response because it is causing problems in their interpersonal and/or work relationships.

It is recommended that after the 12 session group is completed that participants be offered the option of continuing the group. Some of the individuals may opt for individual therapy to continue their exploration or some may wish to begin couples therapy to try to heal their marriage or couple relationship. These options should be afforded to them or appropriate referrals given to them.

The course is based on Cognitive Behavioral Psychology and Solution Focused Therapy Techniques. The course is available ONLINE http:// www.NYMFT.Com), is offered at the Marriage and Family Therapists of New York offices in Rockville Centre, New York (Nassau County,

Long Island) 516-764-2526, and Kerhonkson, New York (Ulster County, New York) 845-626-2257. It is also available as a workshop for sports teams, school health courses, correction and parole officers, mental health clinics, court personnel, judges, attorneys, etc. For more information, please call or email jatwood@optonline.net.

Ongoing Six Month Interaction With Facilitator of Program
The course is interactive in as much as participants have access to a facilitator for six months after they complete the course and can submit questions and receive answers within 24 hours. The purpose of this is to assist participants with setting up and running their first group.

In addition, aside from the information given on Anger Management, participants will be given information on group process—the nuts and bolts of how to run a group, what to look for, how to facilitate.

THE PSYCHOLOGICAL BASIS OF THE PROGRAM

COGNITIVE BEHAVIORAL PSYCHOLOGY (CBT)
Cognitive and/or behavioral psychotherapies (CBP) are psychological approaches based on scientific principles that research has shown to be effective for a wide range of problems. Clients and therapists work together, once a therapeutic alliance has been formed, to identify and understand problems in terms of the relationship between thoughts, feelings and behavior. The approach usually focuses on difficulties in the here and now, and relies on the therapist and client developing a shared view of the individual's problem. This then leads to identification of personalized, usually time-limited therapy goals and strategies, which are continually monitored and evaluated. The treatments are inherently empowering in nature, the outcome being to focus on specific psychological and practical skills (e.g. in reflecting on and exploring the meaning attributed to events and situations and re-evaluation of those meanings) aimed at enabling clients to tackle their problems by harnessing their own resources. The acquisition and utilization of such skills is seen as the main goal, and the active component in

promoting change with an emphasis on putting what has been learned into practice between sessions ("homework"). Thus the overall aim is for the individual to attribute improvement in their problems to their own efforts, in collaboration with the psychotherapist.

Cognitive psychology is a theoretical perspective that focuses on the realms of human perception, thought, and memory. It portrays learners as active processors of information--a metaphor borrowed from the computer world--and assigns critical roles to the knowledge and perspective students bring to their learning. What learners do to enrich information, in the view of cognitive psychology, determines the level of understanding they ultimately achieve.

Vygotsky (1978) emphasized the role of social interactions in knowledge construction. Social constructivism turns attention to children's interactions with parents, peers, and teachers in homes, neighborhoods, and schools. Vygotsky introduced the concept of the *zone of proximal development*, which is the difference between the difficulty level of a problem a client can cope with independently and the level that can be accomplished with help from others. In the zone of proximal development, a client and a therapist work together on problems that the student alone could not work on successfully.

Cognitive and/or behavioral psychotherapists work with individuals, families and groups. The approaches can be used to help anyone irrespective of ability, culture, race, gender or sexual preference.

Underlying Theory of Cognitive Therapy

The central insight of cognitive therapy as originally formulated over three decades ago is that thoughts mediate between stimuli, such as external events, and emotions. As in the figure below, a stimulus elicits a thought -- which might be an evaluative judgment of some kind -- which in turn gives rise to an emotion. In other words, it is not the stimulus *itself* which somehow elicits an emotional response directly, but our evaluation of or thought about that stimulus. Two ancillary assumptions underpin the approach of the cognitive therapist:

- the client is capable of becoming aware of his or her own thoughts and of changing them, and
- sometimes the thoughts elicited by stimuli distort or otherwise fail to reflect reality accurately.

Event Definition of the Situation ❏ Emotion and Behavior

Some Cognitive Behavioral Therapy Principles:

Behavior is Learned
All behavior is learned and just as it was learned it can be unlearned.

Reinforcement
A reinforcer is anything that increases the probability that a behavior will occur. Behavior that is reinforced is likely to occur more frequently. The client defines the reinforcer.

Goals
Therapist and client set up goals for the therapy. Therapy becomes a structured situation whereby client takes action steps toward accomplishing the goals of therapy.

Shaping and Successive Approximations
The way to work toward a terminal behavior is to reinforce baby steps toward that behavior. So that anything that approximates the goal or terminal behavior is reinforced.

Thoughts Lead To Feelings
An event occurs. Based on our early childhood socialization and ongoing socialization, we define the event. Based on that definition, we experience thoughts and feelings. Based on those thoughts and feelings, we behave or act. Actions have consequences. Behaviors that

have positive outcomes tend to be repeated. Behaviors that have negative outcomes tend not to be replicated.

Distorted Thoughts Lead to Negative Communication

Faulty thinking needs to be debunked and changed. There are many ways we distort our thinking. These must be worked on. There are specific techniques for changing distorted thinking.

Positive Self-Talk

Negative thinking and negative communication often gets us into trouble with ourselves or with others. Positive self-talk is a technique that could be used to change negative thinking.

Positive Action

While the therapist and client will "talk" to each other, the focus is on action. Doing things that will make you get closer to your goals and thus help you to feel better.

Contracts

Often therapist and client or client and family or client with himself or herself will design a contract that will help him or her accomplish goals.

SOLUTION FOCUSED BRIEF THERAPY

From Wikipedia - https://en.wikipedia.org/wiki/Solution-focused_brief_therapy

Solution Focused Brief Therapy (SFBT) (often referred to as simply 'solution focused therapy' or 'brief therapy') is a type of talking therapy based upon social constructionist philosophy. It focuses on the clients' therapeutic goals rather than on their problem(s). The approach focuses on the present and future – not the past. The therapist takes a curious approach to help the client envision their preferred future so they may collaborate to create incremental steps toward their goals. To aid the client, questions are asked to highlight their strengths and resources, focusing on exceptions to the problem.

Solution focused therapists believe that change is constant. SFBT therapist help their clients create a version of their preferred future by helping them identify not only what they want to change but also what they want to maintain. The therapist then shifts to shed awareness on times in their life that are closer to this vision – the exceptions. Once these small successes are highlighted the therapist can help the client repeat these different behaviors they take when the problem is less severe, thus helping the client move toward their identified preferred future.

Miracle Question
The miracle question is a technique used to aid the client in visualizing how the future will be different when the problem no longer exists and creating incremental goals to achieve this. A traditional version of the miracle question would go like this: There are many different versions of the miracle question depending on the context and the client. For instance, a therapist can ask: "If I were to wave a magic wand and when you woke up tomorrow a miracle happened so that you no longer easily lost your temper, what would you see differently?" What would the first signs be that the miracle occurred?"

The client may respond by saying, "I would not get upset when someone calls me names."

The therapist wants the client to develop concrete step-by-step goals that determine what will be done versus what they will not do – to ensure success. The therapist may ask, "What will you do instead when someone calls you names?"

Scaling Questions
Scaling questions are tools used to identify quantifiable differences for the client to aid in goal setting. The ends of the scale can be structured as "the worst the problem has ever been" (zero to one) to "the best things could ever be" (ten). The client is asked to rate their current position on the scale, and the therapist follows up with questions to help identify

the client's resources (e.g. "what's stopping you from slipping one point lower down the scale?"), exceptions (e.g. "on a day when you are one point higher on the scale, how can you tell?"), and to describe a preferred future (e.g. "where on the scale is good enough? What would that day look like?").

Exception Seeking Questions

Advocates of SFBT insist there are always times when the problem is less severe or absent for the client. The therapist seeks to encourage the client to describe those different circumstances in those cases as well as what they did differently. The goal is for the client to repeat what worked previously and empower them to make improvements for the future.

Coping Questions

Coping questions are designed to elicit information about client resources that will have gone unnoticed by them. Coping questions are designed to unearth information about client's resources that are under the radar. Even the most hopeless story is latent with examples of coping: "I can see things have been difficult for you, yet I am struck by the fact that you still manage to get up each morning and do everything necessary to send the kids off to school. How do you do that?" Genuine curiosity and admiration can help highlight strengths without appearing to contradict the clients view of reality. The initial summary "I can see that things have been difficult for you" is true for the client and validates their story. The second part "you still manage to get up each morning etc.", is also true, but one that counters the problem focused narrative. Undeniably, they cope and the coping questions start to gently supportively challenge the problem-focused narrative.

Resources

A key task in SFBT is to help clients identify and use their skills, abilities and external resources. This helps construct a narrative of the client as a competent individual and aims to help them identify new ways of bringing these resources to endure the problem. Resources can be identified through the aforementioned techniques. SFBT has branched out in numerous spectrums – most notable, the field of Addiction Counseling utilizes SFBT as an effective means to treat problem drinking.

Thus the Anger Management Program is a blend of the two approaches to therapy. The main assumptions of this approach are:

- The focus is on the here and now.
- The problem or issue-in-living the person is experiencing is learned.
- Just as it was learned, it can be unlearned.
- They have tried many ways to solve their problem—all to no avail.
- Therapy is a relationship between client and therapist.
- Client defines the goal and the therapist assists with achieving the goal.
- Therapy involves mobilizing individual's resources and strengths to seeing new solutions.
- Therapy is brief, solution focused, goal oriented, utilizing behavioral principles.
- Regarding anger, individuals experience anger because they have learned to express anger in this manner.
- By getting to know the thoughts people tell themselves about certain situations and the meanings they give to the thoughts, they then feel a certain way. Thus, an event in the external world occurs. Individuals give that event a certain definition and meaning. These definitions and meanings then lead to the individual feeling a certain way. If the feeling is anger, then individuals will behave in an angry way.
- Behavior has consequences. Anger responses have consequences—both positive and negative. The negative consequences of the anger response far outweigh the positive consequences.

- Just as individuals learned the angry response, they can unlearn it.
- Learning new skills that replace the inappropriate ones help individuals unlearn the response.

*****

Model of Human Behavior

At this point a model of human behavior can be presented. There is socialization from birth until death. There is early childhood socialization by our early caretakers, usually parents. There is also on-going socialization in the schools we attend, the jobs we hold. These are the inputs to how we see the world. They are constantly changing and modified. They are what give us our world views and our belief systems. Based on our world view, an event happens and we define the situation. Based on how we define the situation, we experience feelings. These feelings lead us then to behave in certain ways. Behavior has consequences and the consequences of behavior feed back into our world views and definition of the situation.

An example of this is how our parents handle stress and anxiety will influence how we then handle stress and anxiety. Based on our early childhood socialization, we learn to define certain situation as stressful and we react to that situation in stressful ways. Parents are not the only inputs to our behavior and as we mature, other influences impinge on our world view. Maybe we will incorporate other situations as stressful or maybe there will be a decrease in the number of situations that we define as stressful. Our world view is constantly being influenced. If the community in which we live condones roughhousing of women, we .learn to condone it also. So if we watch a woman being roughed up by her husband, we may see that as a typical situation. "Well she had it coming to her." Based on that definition, we might do nothing to help her. But say for example we get a job in a safe house and we get a full view of women's feelings and experiences of being abused. Well then, there is another input to our behavior. Perhaps this input will be salient enough for us to alter our worldview somewhat. Perhaps we become not as accepting of women being roughed around. The next time we are in that situation where we witness a woman being pushed or shoved, our response might be agitation. We might even act to try to stop the encounter. Our world view was altered by incoming socialization. This altered how we defined the situation which in turn caused us to experience certain feelings. Then we acted differently than we did the first time.

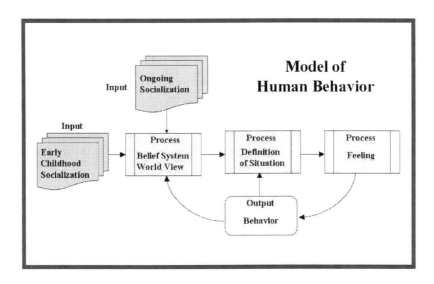

THE ANGER MANAGEMENT
PROFESSIONAL CERTIFICATION PROGRAM

The Program:

This Program is to help you help individuals recognize and manage anger and its expression. It will provide you with information so that you will be able to better understand the anger response and in so doing specialize in anger management, whether it be working with individuals or on a group basis.

Group Objectives:

At the end of your training and the subsequent implementation, your clients and/or your students will be able to do the following:

* They will recognize their own role in the management and control of their emotions.
* They will understand their anger response, as well as their stress response.
* They will be able to recognize their anger cues or situation that invite them to be angry that can lead to violent behavior.
* They will learn skills to control their angry responses and to reduce the stress in their lives.
* They will learn communication skills and listening skills that will enable them to effectively communicate their feelings to others.

Group Rules:
- **Group Safety:** No violence or threats of violence toward staff or other group members are permitted. It is important that clients view the group as a safe place where they can share their experiences and feelings without threats or fear of physical harm. It is expected that all group members will share their experiences.
- **Confidentiality**: Group members should not discuss outside of the group anything that was discussed in the group. Anything

a group member says must be kept within the group and not discussed anyplace else.

- **Drugs/Alcohol:** Any member who appears to be under the influence of drugs and/or alcohol will be dismissed from the group.
- **Crosstalk:** When someone is talking, others are respectful and remain quiet until the person is finished with his or her thought. Each person should have a chance to talk.
- **Homework Assignments:** Each week brief homework assignments are given. Doing the homework assignments helps to create continuity between sessions and will improve the members' anger management skills and help them obtain the most from the group experience.
- **Derogatory Comments:** No derogatory, racial, or ethnic statements will be accepted in the group. No profanity is permitted.
- **Fees:** All fees for group sessions must be paid at time of session. No certificate of completion will be given to members who have outstanding bills.
- **Absences and Cancellations:** Group members are expected to arrive to class on time. Group members should call or notify the group leader in advance if they cannot attend a group session. Because of the amount of material presented in each session, no more than two sessions are permitted.

If a member misses more than two sessions, they are permitted to attend the weekly sessions but will not be given the certificate of completion.

* **Timeouts:** If the group leader feels that a member is losing control, s/he may call a time out at any time. Eventually a group member may call a time out themselves if they feel that they are losing control.

Individual and Group Responsibilities:
- Individuals will keep a daily anger and stress journal.
- They will identify when they are angry and when they are stressed.
- They will identity when they are in a potentially angry situation or when they are in a potentially stressful situation.
- They will hone in on their own angry feelings and stress feelings.
- They will notice what their anger buttons are.
- They will learn to recognize the early warning signals of their anger response.
- They will learn the skills necessary to reduce the stress in their lives and get control over their anger response.
- They will learn communication skills necessary to effectively communicate emotions so that they can keep themselves under control.

Attendance:

Usually there are 12 sessions to an Anger Management Program. If more are necessary or individual therapy is indicated, then persons should be guided accordingly. At other times, persons in individual therapy might be guided into an anger management group to practice the learned skills. In either case, attendance should be kept and persons should receive a Certificate of Completion if they have completed at a minimum 10 of the 12 sessions.

ATTENDANCE FORM

NAME _____

ADDRESS _____

PHONE (Home and Cell) _____

EMAIL _____

EMERGENCY CONTACT: _____

ATTENDANCE

	Present	**Absent**

Session 1
Date _____
Session 2
Date _____
Session 3
Date _____
Session 4
Date _____
Session 5
Date _____
Session 6
Date _____
Session 7
Date _____
Session 8
Date _____
Session 9
Date _____
Session 10
Date _____

Session 11

Date _____

Session 12

Date _____

RESEARCH

If you are interested in doing research in terms of program evaluation and effectiveness, there are several instruments that can be used to effectively measure pre and post program responses.

Some of these instruments are:
Thomas Kilman Conflict Mode Instrument
Barret Impulsivity Scale (BIS-11)

MODULE II

MAKING FRIENDS WITH YOUR ANGER

ANGER

What is Anger?

Anger is an emotional state that varies in intensity from mild irritation and annoyance to intense fury and rage. Anger is not aggression.

What is Aggression?

Aggression is behavior that is intended to cause harm or to do damage to a person or property.

What is Hostility?

Hostility is a set of attitudes, ideas, and judgments that tend to motivate aggression.

What is Stress?

Stress is a reaction to situations, events or people. Usually when we speak of stress we are usually describing a set of symptoms that vary from person to person (upset stomach, nervous feelings, headaches, and other symptoms.

What Causes Anger?
Anger is caused by a host of reasons. Some are:

- We have learned to express anger. We watched our parents get angry. This is the way they resolved issues, so we are likely to use the same approach.
- We tell ourselves negative self-talk that create feelings that lead us to define places, people, and things as problematic. The basic premise is that thoughts lead to feelings that lead to behavior.
- If we are stressed or frustrated we are likely to feel anger.
- If we are tired or hungry, we are likely to react in an angry way.

Getting to Know Your Anger

Do people tell you need to calm down? Or not to yell or curse so much?

Do you feel tense most of the time?

Do you find yourself "stuffing" your angry feelings and then exploding over something small?

Do you find yourself not saying what's on your mind most of the time when you're at school or at work or in your relationship?

Do you feel the only way people will listen to you is if you yell?

When you are upset about something, do you do behaviors that help you block it out of your mind? Like watching TV, sleeping a lot, reading books or magazines?

Are you drinking or drugging daily to help calm you down?

Do you have a problem sleeping because you are agitated?

Do you feel unheard or misunderstood much of the time?

Do your loved ones tell you that you hurt them and your friends are not calling as much?

YOUR ANGER RATING WORKSHEET

In the next section, you will get to know your anger. This will help you to manage it. Please keep in mind that we use a multi-pronged approach to managing anger. Getting to know your anger is one prong. Examining your negative cognitions and how you then define people, places and things according to those cognitions will also be explored in later sections.

What is Your Anger Rating?

Use a 1 to 10 scale. A score of 1 represents a complete lack of anger. A score of 10 represents an angry and explosive loss of control that generally leads to negative consequences.

Total 0_____	1-2-3_____	4-5-6_____	10 Violence
State of	Irritated	Agitated	Exploding
Calm	Annoyed	Mad	Rage
	Bothered	Pissed-Off	Out of Control

If your responses were in the 0-2 range, you anger is manageable, although you may benefit from Anger Management Training,

If your responses were between 3-5, your anger is moderate. You need to learn more about what stresses you out and then develop stress management techniques, which would be covered in our anger management program.

If your responses were 6 and over, your anger is out of control. You have an anger problem that could benefit from learning anger management techniques.

THE ANGER LOG
WORKSHEET

Keep an anger log for a week. List the days of the week and for each day of the week, list your anger rating. Be prepared to report to the group the following week on what you learned.

The anger log is separated into columns.

The first column is called Pain and Frustration. Here you record your emotional and physical pain that existed right before your anger. Maybe it would be anxiety over your marriage or a headache. Maybe you be worried about an examination that you would be taking. Maybe you thought your girlfriend lied to you.

The next column, provocative situation, is where you would briefly record the event that triggered your anger. Here you would write, possibly hearing that one of your wife's friends is getting divorced, or the realization that you didn't study for your test and now there was no more time, or your girlfriend sounding funny to you on the phone when you asked her where she was last night.

The next column, trigger thoughts, is where you record what you were thinking before you expressed your anger. Here you would record whatever thoughts you were giving yourself, such as maybe now your wife will want a divorce, the thought that you might fail the course, the idea that maybe your girlfriend was cheating on you.

The fourth column, anger rating, is where you record your anger rating between 0 and 10.

The fifth column, your behavior, is where you would record what you actually did as a response to your anger.

The sixth column, outcomes, is where you would record the effect of your anger—on yourself and on others. Use separate sheets if necessary. Be prepared to discuss your log with the group or your therapist.

Feel free to Xerox the sheet or use additional sheets if necessary.

THE ANGER LOG
WORKSHEET

Anger Event	Pain Frustration	Provocative Situation	Trigger Thoughts	Anger Rating	Your Behavior	Outcomes
1.						
2.						
3.						
4.						
5.						
6.						
7.						

NOTES

HOW YOU LOOK WHEN YOU ARE ANGRY
WORKSHEET

People look all different ways when they are angry. How do you look when you are angry? Do the veins in your neck bulge? Is your face beet red? Is your face all gnarled and twisted? What does your body look like? What are you doing with your hands?

Describe in words how you look when you are angry.

_____

_____

_____

_____

_____

Now, below, as best as you could, draw a picture of how you look when you are angry.

SOME CONSEQUENCES OF ANGER
WORKSHEET

In this section, you will explore the consequences of your anger—Some consequences are positive and you will explore those. But most are negative and you will explore those. Be as specific as you can in your answers.

Anger has some positive consequences in that it releases tension and tends to get people to do what you want for the moment. What are some of the positive consequences of your anger?

_____

_____

_____

_____

_____

There are anger payoffs. What are your anger payoffs? To reduce stress? Using anger to discharge stress related arousal? Write down your anger payoffs.

_____

_____

_____

_____

_____

Some people use anger to hide Emotional Pain? Do you? Do you use anger to defend against shame, guilt, depression, anxiety, feelings of vulnerability? Write down the emotions you feel when you do this.

_____

_____

_____

_____

_____

Do you use anger to get attention? Or do you use anger to alarm people so they will listen to you? Write down the emotions you can relate to when you do this.

_____

_____

_____

_____

_____

Do you use anger as a punishment and revenge? Do you use anger to make people feel as much pain as you do? Write down what you feel when you do this.

_____

_____

_____

_____

_____

Or do you use anger to change the behavior of others? To coerce people to do what you want? Write down what you feel when you do this.

_____

_____

_____

_____

_____

The above tend to be short term consequences. Generally anger has long term negative consequences that far outweigh the positive consequences. What are some of the negative consequences of your anger?

_____

_____

_____

_____

_____

The worst anger occurs between people who are close to us. We always hurt the ones we love or so the song goes. How has your anger hurt your family of origin relationships, including parents, siblings, and extended family?

_____

_____

_____

_____

_____

How has anger affected your marriage or intimate/romantic, relationships?

_____

_____

_____

_____

_____

How has your anger affected your children?

_____

_____

_____

_____

_____

Work also provides us with situations that can create anger. Bosses, co-workers, teachers, customers, deadlines, unfairness—all these can take a toll on our patience. What are some ways your anger has hurt your work or school relationships?

_____

_____

_____

_____

_____

How has your anger affected your friendships (including lost friends and/or strained relationships)?

_____

_____

_____

_____

_____

How has your anger harmed people who aren't family or friends. Include the names of all the people your anger has hurt? Use a separate sheet if necessary.

_____

_____

_____

_____

_____

How has your anger affected your health and physical well being (including stress-related illnesses/problems and physical discomfort from anger reactions)?

_____

_____

_____

_____

_____

How has your anger endangered you (including reckless driving, physical fights, hurting yourself by hitting things, legal problems, etc)?

_____

_____

_____

_____

How has anger affected you financially (include bad decisions made in a rage, material things broken or damaged)?

_____

_____

_____

_____

_____

How has your anger affected you spiritually (including bad behavior that goes against your personal code of ethics or sense of right and wrong)?

_____

_____

_____

_____

_____

How has your anger affected how you feel about yourself?

_____

_____

_____

_____

_____

Dr. Joan D. Atwood

Facts:

As our anger goes up, our IQ goes down.

When we are angry, we are unreasonable.

When we are angry, we are more likely to do dangerous things.

Anger is the wind that blows out the lamp of the mind.
Robert Ingersoll

To Sum Up:

What is Anger?

Anger is a human emotion. It is natural and everyone feels angry from time to time. Feeling angry sometimes is normal, but no one can make you feel angry. You are the one who decides how you feel. While it is OK to feel angry, it is NOT OK to feel aggressive or violent.

What Causes Anger?

There are many reasons why people become angry. Mainly though, anger is connected to how you think and feel.

Generally speaking, the way you behave when you are angry is based on what you have learned in life. Be aware that just as you learned behaviors, you can "unlearn" behaviors also. Anger can sometimes get you into trouble. You can unlearn these behaviors that get you into trouble by learning new behaviors when you are angry that will not get you into trouble.

What Does Anger Do To Your Body?

Anger affects your body in many different ways. It increases adrenaline and other chemicals into the blood stream which causes the heart to pump faster, raises the blood pressure, tenses the muscles, causes dry mouth, upsets the stomach, causes sweating and basically causes a "flight or flight" reaction.

Generally speaking, the way anger affects the body is usually not harmful, but it could be if a person is angry for long periods of time. Being angry over a long period of time can cause a host of health problems, not to mention relationship problems with those around you. No one wants to be around an angry person. To avoid this, it is wise to learn to control your anger.

MODULE III

THE PHYSIOLOGY OF ANGER AND STRESS

Speak when you are angry and you will make
the best speech you will ever regret.
Laurence J. Peter

THE PHYSIOLOGY OF ANGER AND STRESS

Stress is intricately interwoven with Anger. When you define a situation as angry, certain physical symptoms occurs. Our bodies go into what is called flight or fight reactions. This is controlled by the sympathetic portion of our autonomic nervous system, specifically the sympathetic portion. Powerful hormones (adrenaline) associated with stress are secreted into your body. This is an emergency reaction and its purpose is to prepare you to fight or to flight (run away). This response is a carryover from thousands of yeas ago when there were dangerous animals lurking.

When your brain registers an emergency situation, the hormone adrenaline is secreted into your bloodstream. This creates certain physiological things to happen:

- Blood is shifted to the muscles and your skin becomes pale.
- Your body begins to prepare itself to run, and you start to sweat.
- Your heart rate goes up.
- Your blood pressure rises.
- Your pupils dilate.
- Your body prepares itself for increased fuel demands by releasing glucose and fatty acids into your blood stream.
- Your immune system slows down, because energy is shifted to anticipate the battle rather than maintain health.

What symptoms have you noticed in yourself when you are angry or under a lot of stress?

_____
_____
_____
_____
_____
_____
_____

Can you identify the stressors in your life? Persons, Places, Situations?

_____

_____

_____

_____

_____

_____

_____

The Stress Symptom Checklist on the next page will help you notice what your stress level is. Add up your score after checking off your symptoms and you will see if your stress level is low, moderate, high, or very high.

Let me empathize once again that in this portion of the workbook, you will intimately work toward getting to know your anger and your stress. In later sections you will examine your cognitions—your thoughts—in terms of negative or distorted thinking. This is another prong of our approach.

On the following page, there is a **Stress Worksheet** that will help you to monitor when your stressful periods are during the day. You will be able to see if you are most stressed at night or in the morning or in the afternoon. You will also be able to see what the situations are that make you stressed.

Life Cycle Changes, sudden changes, good or bad, cause stress. A person by the name of Holmes created a **Life Stress Inventory, which** is a helpful test to assist you in learning to understand your stressors. Knowing your stressors can help you reduce them in your life. AND reducing the stress n your life will help to reduce your anger.

Sometimes increased stress energizes us:
- We feel increased motivation and drive
- We experience a sense of challenge and excitement

- We feel a sense of renewed energy
- We can focus on detail, and accuracy
- We have feelings of excitement and hope
- We have increased self-confidence

However, there is a very unhealthy side of stress and it affects us in four (4) major ways:

1. Changes in our bodies
2. Changes in our thinking
3. Unhealthy or distorted thinking
4. Changes in our emotions or over-stimulated emotions
5. Changes in our actions

1. Changes in Your Body:
There are profound changes in our body. These are short term changes and long term changes.

Short Term Changes:
- Faster heart rate
- Cool skin
- Rapid breathing
- Dry mouth
- Diarrhea
- Increased sweating
- Cold hands and feet
- Tense muscles
- A desire to urinate
- Butterflies in your stomach

What kinds of short term physical changes have you noticed in yourself as a result of your increased stress level?

_____
_____
_____

_____

_____

_____

_____

Long Term Changes:
These occur when your body has been exposed to adrenaline over a long period of time. One of the ways that adrenaline prepares you for action is by diverting resources to the muscles from the areas of the body which carry out body maintenance. This means that if you are exposed to adrenaline for a sustained period, then your health might start to deteriorate. This may show up in the following ways:

- Changes in appetite
- Increase or decrease in weight
- Asthma
- Headaches
- Sexual disorders
- Feelings of intense and long term tiredness/fatigue
- Frequent colds
- Digestive problems
- Skin eruptions
- Aches and pains
- Anxiety or depression

What kinds of long term physical changes have you noticed in yourself as a result of your increased stress level?

_____

_____

_____

_____

_____

_____

2. Changes in Your Thinking:
- Trouble concentrating
- Lost self-confidence
- Lapses of memory
- Poor Judgment
- Feeling pressured

Discuss any changes in your thinking that have occurred as a result of your increased stress level.

_____

_____

_____

_____

_____

_____

_____

3. Changes in Your Emotions:
- Resentment
- Anger and Irritability
- Feeling "on edge" or agitated
- Feeling blue, down in the dumps, hopeless
- Moodiness

Discuss any changes in your emotions that you have noticed as a result of increased stress.

_____

_____

_____

_____

_____

_____

_____

4. Changes in Your Actions/Behavior:

- Increased smoking behavior
- Increased drugging or alcohol behavior
- Increased violence, throwing things, punching holes in walls, pushing someone, etc.
- Withdrawing from others
- Non-Stop Talking
- Fidgeting
- Absenteeism

Discuss any changes in your behaviors that you have noticed as a result of your increased stress level.

_____

_____

_____

_____

_____

_____

_____

Since stress and anger affect you in four different ways, as you will see later, our approach to managing your stress and anger will be a four pronged approach.

Research Studies Have Shown Over and Over Again

*There is a connection between unexpressed
anger and hypertension.*

There is a connection between expressed anger and hypertension.

*There is a connection between anger, hostility and various
forms of cardiovascular disease.*

*There is a connection between anger, hostility and
total mortality (death).*

*There is a connection between anger, hostility and
less satisfying social supports.*

*There is a connection between anger,
hostility and damaged friendships,
increased fights with family members, and
difficulties in school and/or in the workplace.*

Substances That Increase Stress:
Abusing any substance whatsoever is a guaranteed way to increase your stress level. Drug abuse problems involving opiates (heroin, Demerol, dragon) and the major stimulants (speed, cocaine, crack, nicotine, and caffeine) are beyond the scope of this program. If these substances, including alcohol, are having an adverse affect on your life in terms of affecting your behavior at work, your personal relationships and your health, then it is important to see someone who specializes in this area, i.e. drug abuse counselor.

REDUCING STRESS

Relaxation
Everyone will benefit from stress reducing techniques. There are many of them. There are tapes that you can purchase.

If you don't have a tape, try these exercises. Go to a quiet place. Sit in a comfortable chair. Get comfortable. Dim the lights.

- Take a deep breath; hold it to the count of three.
- Slowly let it out while mentally thinking "relax."
- Take another deep breath; hold it to the count of three.
- Slowly let it out while mentally thinking the word "relax."
- Tighten both fists; count to three.
- Open your fists and relax.
- Take another deep breath; hold it to the count of three.
- Slowly let it out while thinking the word "relax."

Progressive Muscle Relaxation
- Sit in a quiet place in a comfortable chair.
- Dim the lights.
- Beginning with your left foot, tighten the muscles. Clench your left foot.
- Focus on the tension building up in your left foot.
- Release it.
- Now focus on the tension flowing out.
- Do the same thing with your right foot.
- Now work up your body with all your large muscle groupings.
- Tense then relax your left calf, right calf, left thigh, right thigh, buttocks, stomach muscles, left fist, right fist, left bicep, right bicep, shoulders, neck and face.
- Pay special attention to your shoulders, neck and face area as tension and stress seem to build up in these areas.

The entire process should take about 15-20 minutes. When you complete this exercise, you should be in a deep state of muscle relaxation.

These exercises will help you to notice when you are beginning to stress up and when you are relaxed and also, with practice, how you can get from one state to another.

A Positive Moment

While sitting in the chair in the quiet room, remember a moment of success that you experienced. Go over your thoughts as you accomplished what you had to accomplish—the hard work, the planning, etc. Then put yourself at the moment of completion—the point when you looked at the finished product and/or finished your project and knew that it was a job well done. Stay with the moment and re-experience it.

Visual Imagery

Some people are more visual than physical and visual imagery works better for them. While sitting in the comfortable chair with the lights dimmed, picture yourself a tree. Focus on the details of the tree—the leaves, the tree trunk, the different colors. Picture your anxiety in the tree. Usually people make the anxiety red, but make it any color you would like. Now with a broom, a mop, a squeegee or any tool you would like, go into the tree and start pushing the anxiety up and out through the trunk, through the branches and out. Do this work in your mind's eye until all the red (your anxiety) is pushed out of the tree.

Gaining Control Over Stress

Stress is a preexisting condition to Anger. Reducing the stress in your life will help you reduce the anger. Think about the stressful situations in your life. Make a list of the situations and people that create stress for you.

_____

_____

_____

_____

_____

How to Reduce Immediate Stress

Some Helpful Suggestions:

Intense Work Activity
Chores like washing the dishes, vacuuming, cooking, exercising, walking, painting, fixing and building all function to reduce stress by channeling your energy into a focused task.

Humor
We very often ignore the importance of humor in our lives. Looking at the light side. "Lighten up" is the expression to use for yourself. Poke fun at things. Reframe your stress into something much less serious. Try not to take yourself so seriously. Imagine those causing you stress on the toilet, slipping on a banana peel, etc.

Writing
Writing in a journal reduces stress It is an effective way of reducing stress and getting feelings out. It also provides you with a record of your progress.

Recreation
Reading, TV, games, and hobbies can act as psychological sponges that soak up stress.

Verbalizing Pain
Talking about your pain can reduce your stress. There is evidence that talking about what is on your mind helps you to categorize it and work on logically solving the problems associated with it. Language forces us to logically and coherently order our sentences etc., so that when we verbally discuss things, there is a tendency to work some things through, to get others' opinions, and also to decrease some of the emotion attached to the problem. This will work up to a point when further talking about the problem serves to reinforce it.

Sex

Sex turns on your parasympathetic nervous system, which is antagonistic to the sympathetic nervous system, the nervous system responsible for your flight or flight reaction and your anxiety/stress response. So that when the parasympathetic system is on (and it is during sex, during digestion and during relaxation), the sympathetic system is off.

Problem Solving Activities

Any steps toward solving some of your problems serves to reduce stress.

Problem Solving Communication

Calmly expressing your needs can help to reduce stress. This can be expressed to a therapist or your partner or friend.

Music

Music can be profoundly calming. Use whatever music you like and listen to it for a while. It is a sure-bet stress reducer.

Resting

Have a period of no activity. Go to bed and watch TV or just lie there resting.

Yoga and Massage

Take up yoga and massage.

Which of the above do you already do to reduce your stress?

_____

_____

_____

_____

_____

Which of the above would you like to incorporate into your life?

_____

_____

_____

_____

_____

What can you do in the next week that would reduce the stress and anxiety in your life? Be very specific. List some things that are on the above list and/or some very specific things that you can do that are not on the list.

_____

_____

_____

_____

_____

Reducing your stress level will directly reduce your likelihood of having an angry attack. In addition, these techniques that you use for stress reduction are the exact techniques that you can utilize to reduce your anger response.

These and the remainder of the exercises in the book are relatively simple exercises. It is important to practice them so that you can then call upon them as your anger starts to rise.

MODULE IV

PRECEDING EVENTS: CORE BELIEFS TRIGGERING EVENTS IMPULSES

PRECEEDING EVENTS:
CORE BELIEFS

Tranquility is Not Freedom from the storm
but Peace Within the storm ...

In the following modules you will begin to examine the preceding events to your anger. In this way you get to know your specific anger response. These are important because all too often people think their anger response is instantaneous and that when they experience it, it is full blown. As you will learn in the following sections, there are many events that take place prior to a full blown anger attack. Knowing about the very early cues will help you to stop your anger response earlier and earlier.

PLEASE NOTE:
IT IS NOT NECESSARILY THE PRECEDING
EVENTS WHICH TRIGGER OUR ANGER. IT IS
RATHER HOW WE DEFINE THESE EVENTS—
THE MEANING WE GIVE THESE EVENTS.

CORE BELIEFFS

What are Core Beliefs?

- Core beliefs are lifelong patterned attitudes and beliefs that organize our experience of ourselves and the world.
- We accept them as true and we don't question them. They are rigid.
- They tend to operate in very subtle ways, usually out of our awareness. For example, if you have a core belief that you are stupid, then you wouldn't apply for a job that requires a lot of thinking.
- We tend to be drawn to situations in adult life that trigger our core beliefs, even though they were created in childhood. We

are comfortable with our belief system. This doesn't mean that we would not want to change it. It just means that we are used to the belief; we are familiar with it.

- Generally there is a lot of emotion tied to the core beliefs.
- These beliefs are difficult to work with. It is important to remember that they can change.

These beliefs are part of our meaning system. They tell us what the events happening in these triggering situations mean. So that if we believe that some person is making us feel inadequate, we will feel that way and our behavior will follow.

Common Core Beliefs:

Helpless Core Beliefs

I am helpless	I am inadequate
I am powerless	I am ineffective
I am out of control	I am incompetent
I am weak	I am a failure
I am vulnerable	I am disrespected
I am needy	I am defective
I don't measure up to others	I am trapped
I am not good enough	Everyone should do things as I do

Unlovable Core Beliefs

I am unlovable	I am unworthy
I am unlikable	I am different
I am undesirable	I am defective
Others will not love me	I am not good enough
I am unattractive	I am bound to be rejected
I am uncared for	I am bound to be abandoned
I am a bad person	I am destined to be alone

There are also positive core beliefs. I am a good person. I am intelligent, etc. Think about some of your core beliefs. See if you can pinpoint some entrenched, basic core beliefs that you have. List the positive and negative core beliefs that you have about yourself.

_____

_____

_____

_____

_____

_____

_____

PRECEDING EVENTS:
TRIGGER EVENTS

Now that you have gotten to know your anger, and you have an understanding of your core belief system, you should be ready to define the underlying trigger thoughts that push you to your anger response.

The underlying trigger thoughts for your anger are interwoven with your core beliefs about yourself.

Trigger thoughts fuel our anger. They are the underlying beliefs, the buttons that get pressed right before we exhibit our anger. For example, someone may cut in front of you in traffic and you may experience road rage as a result. The external event is that the person cut in front of you. The internal event could be that s/he was taking advantage of you, was trying to control you, was taking advantage of the situation, etc., It could be a number of things.

People have underlying trigger events that fuel their anger response. They are usually core beliefs that were created when they were little. While we are not going to dwell on how these beliefs originated in the first place, it is useful to know what our trigger buttons are.

Usually a person has a few trigger events. These are related to the core beliefs that can arise in various situations. The buttons can be pushed with loved ones, with authority figures, with strangers. They are our core beliefs that trigger our annoyance, our anger, our rage.

Some examples of underlying anger trigger buttons are:

- I feel taken advantage of.
- I feel not appreciated.
- I feel unloved.
- I feel not cared about.
- No one notices my accomplishments.
- No one understands me.

- No One listens to me.
- Everyone else's' needs are more important than mine.
- I am overlooked.
- I feel that whatever we do, it isn't good enough.
- I feel like I am low man/woman on the totem pole.
- I feel second best to everyone else.

Think back to the last time you were angry, think about what REALLY triggered your anger. Pinpoint and discuss your underlying trigger thoughts

_____

_____

_____

_____

_____

_____

_____

Now keep a trigger log for a week. Monitor your anger response. Whenever you get angry, try to pinpoint the underlying feeling that you experienced.

TRIGGER EVENT
WORKSHEET

Day	Event	Underlying Trigger
Monday		
Tuesday		
Wednesday		
Thursday		
Friday		
Saturday		
Sunday		

Summarize your three most powerful, meaningful triggers—those triggers that get pulled over and over again.

1. _____

2. _____

3. _____

PRECEDING EVENTS:
THE NATURE OF IMPULSES
AND
HOW TO ACHIEVE IMPULSE CONTROL

There is a direct correlation between impulses and anger. Persons who have poor impulse control also have a hard time controlling their anger. In this section, we will learn about impulses—their nature and how to begin to control them.

Goal of This Session:

The goal of the Session is to understand what triggers and causes impulsive behaviors that can be problematic or cause negative consequences for the person and/or for others.

Another goal of the session is to learn specific strategies that persons can use to intervene effectively to manage impulses and help him or her achieve their long terms goals.

Use Barret Impulsivity Scale (BIS-11) to measure impulsivity.

This test was developed with prison populations and it is used to measure persons who have problems with explosive episodes. This is not a standardized test because it was based on a prison population originally but can be used to measure impulsivity. There should be a decrease in the score post treatment if impulsivity was an issue for them. Could also be used during the course of treatment to check progress.

Impulsive Behavior is behavior that occurs:
* without control, inhibition, restraint, or suppression,
* without thinking, reflection, or consideration,
* without foresight, adequate planning, or regard for the consequences,
* or with a sense of immediacy and spontaneity (McCown, JohnSon, and Shore, 1973).

On the next page is a worksheet (Getting to Know Your Impulses) that will help you to get familiar with your impulse response. By getting familiar with all the aspects of your impulse response you can then get control over it. It becomes conscious behavior instead of what feels like a "knee Jerk response."

GETTING TO KNOW YOUR IMPULSES
WORKSHEET

Examples of Impulses: binging, purging, self-mutilation, drugging, throwing things, punching holes in walls, shoving someone, drinking, hitting, stealing etc.

1. Identify your impulse (s).

_____

_____

_____

_____

_____

_____

_____

2. What are the advantages of engaging in this impulsive action? What do you hope to accomplish through this action?

_____

_____

_____

_____

_____

_____

_____

3. What are the disadvantages of engaging in this impulsive behavior?

_____

_____

_____

_____

_____

_____

_____

4. Do you want to control this behavior? Why?

_____

_____

_____

_____

_____

_____

_____

This worksheet will help you identify some thoughts that you had that led up to acting out the impulse.

IMPULSE CONTROL CHART
WORKSHEET

1. Identify a specific impulsive behavior that you wish to control more effectively.

_____

_____

_____

2. Now, think of a specific time when you felt unable to prevent yourself from engaging in the impulsive behavior that you identified above. Complete the following questions based on this particular episode.

_____

_____

_____

3. Before engaging in the particular impulsive behavior…
   what were you thinking?

_____

_____

_____

4. Before engaging in the particular impulsive behavior….
   what were you feeling?

_____

_____

_____

5. Before engaging in the particular impulsive behavior, what external triggers existed?

_____

_____

_____

6. While engaging in the impulsive behavior, what specifically were you doing?

_____

_____

_____

7. While engaging in the specific behavior, what thoughts were running through your head?

_____

_____

_____

8. While engaging in the impulsive behavior… how were you feeling?

_____

_____

_____

9. After engaging in the impulsive behavior… what positive consequences did you experience?

_____

_____

_____

10. After engaging in the impulsive behavior… what negative experiences did you experience?

_____

_____

_____

The above exercise was to help you become more aware of your impulsive behavior and to help you understand that impulsive behavior does "not just happen." There are many preceding events that occur along the way—events that can be interrupted at any point. The purpose of this exercise is to make what feels like reflexive behavior on your part become consciously aware and controlled.

Throughout this book, the suggestions and exercises given to control your anger attacks focus on your physiology, your thoughts and beliefs, your feelings, and your behaviors.

This next worksheet (Ways to Change the Triggers of My Impulse) will assist you in learning what techniques you can use to control your impulses.

WAYS TO CHANGE THE TRIGGERS OF MY IMPULSE

Thoughts: What are some things that you can tell yourself that can make the occurrence of the impulsive behavior less likely?

_____

_____

_____

_____

_____

_____

Feelings: What are some ways you can modify your feelings about the typical triggers for your angry response?

_____

_____

_____

_____

_____

_____

External Triggers: What are some ways that you can change your environment so that you are less likely to act impulsively?

_____

_____

_____

_____

_____

_____

SOME HELPFUL SUGGESTIONS FOR
CONTROLLING IMPULSES

Grounding:
Grounding is a set of techniques that can help you get through moments of extreme emotional pain (above 6 on a 0 to 10 emotional scale, see P. of this booklet), when you are in too much distress to use other coping methods. It is also helpful when dealing with flashbacks, temptations to use substances, or urges to do self-harm. It is a way to delay and distract during a crisis moment and is similar to other techniques like "centering" or finding a "safe place."

Grounding works by anchoring you in the present, concrete reality.

The key to success with grounding is finding what works for you and what you need in the moment. Remember that the idea is to draw your mind away from dangerous chaotic thoughts to safer, concrete thoughts.

Therapists: Please note that this is different from relaxation or positive imagery.

Below are a series of steps that will introduce you to beginning concepts in grounding which will ultimately help to control your anger attacks.

Physical:

The physical is often used as a first step.

Notice your breath. Breathe in through your nose for 4 counts, hold for 4 counts, exhale slowly through your mouth for 4 counts. Repeat 5 times.

Place your feet on the floor; notice the feeling of your feet on the floor and your body in your chair.

Wiggle your toes in your shoes and dig your heels into the floor gently.

Touch your chair. What does it feel like? What color is it? Does it feel cold or warm, smooth or rough?

Find a small object nearby. Hold it in your hand. Say everything you can about it (color, texture, weight).

Clench your fists as tightly as you can for 5 seconds and then release. Press your palms together and do the same. Notice any differences.

Grab onto your chair as tightly as you can, pulling yourself down into it.

Mental/Cognitive:

It is important to tailor these specifically to YOUR needs. Try to find something that is distracting enough to hold your mind in place, but not too overwhelming or frustrating.

Remind yourself where you are, exactly and what day/time it is.

Describe your environment in detail. Name all the colors you see very specifically. Count things in the room (chairs and books).

The above exercises help to keep you focused in the here and now. They will keep your mind from wandering.

Skills for Reducing Impulsive Behavior:

- **Delay Strategies:** When a person puts off engaging in an impulsive behavior, the urge to do the behavior usually decreases.

1. Stop and Think:
2. Count backwards from 10 slowly. Count backwards from 100 by 3s. 100, 97, 94 etc.
3. Delay responding for a set period of time before engaging in the impulsive behavior. During this delay, you may engage in a number of distracting behaviors such as those discussed above.

- **Distraction Strategies:** Distracting yourself is doing something that takes your mind off of your impulsive urge. Choose activities that are enjoyable to you and also are incompatible with the impulsive behavior. Create a list of distracting activities when you are not feeling impulsive. Then when you feel an impulsive urge, repeat the distracting activities on your list until the urge subsides.
  1. Call a friend/sponsor instead of drugging,
  2. Exercise instead of drinking.
  3. Take a walk or run around the block when you feel the urge to act this way toward someone.
  4. Listen to music or write in your journal instead of giving into destructive urges.

To Sum Up....

- Thus far you have learned about your anger.
- You have learned about your anger response.
- You are now aware of the physiological changes that happen to you when you are angry.
- You have looked at the stressors in your life that can contribute to your anger.
- You have explored the preceding events to your anger so that you can begin to recognize when you are getting angry earlier and earlier.

NOTES

MODULE V

THE CYCLE OF VIOLENCE AND THE AGGRESSION RESPONSE

If you kick a stone in anger, you will hurt your foot.
Chinese Philosopher

THE CYCLE OF VIOLENCE AND
THE AGGRESSION RESPONSE

- Every six hours a woman is murdered at the hands of her partner.
- Every 9 seconds, a woman is battered by her spouse.
- More than 50% of all murder victims are killed by an intimate partner.
- Thirty nine per cent of emergency room visits by women are due to domestic violence.
- Among women aged 15-44 years, domestic violence is the leading cause of injury.

WHAT IS DOMESTIC VIOLENCE?

Domestic violence is about one person getting and keeping power and control over another person in an intimate relationship. The abusive person might be your current or former spouse, live-in lover or dating partner. A psychologist and law school professor who is an expert in domestic violence has described it as "a pattern of behavior in which one intimate partner uses physical violence, coercion, threats, intimidation, isolation and emotional, sexual or economic abuse to control and change the behavior of the other partner." (Mary Ann Dutton)

Domestic violence happens to people of all ages, races, ethnicities, and religions. It occurs in both opposite-sex and same-sex relationships. Economic or professional status does not indicate domestic violence - abusers and victims can be laborers or college professors, judges or janitors, doctors or orderlies, schoolteachers, truck drivers, homemakers or store clerks. Domestic violence occurs in the poorest ghettos, the fanciest mansions and white-picket-fence neighborhoods.

About 95% of victims of domestic violence are women. Over 50% of all women will experience physical violence in an intimate relationship, and for 24-30% of those women, the battering will be regular and on-going. Every 15 seconds the crime of battering occurs. (National

Coalition Against Domestic Violence General Information Packet). Most abusers are men. They may seem gentle, mean, quiet or loud, and may be big or small. There is some evidence that shows boys who grow up with domestic violence often become abusers as adults, however, many abusers are from non-violent homes, and many boys from violent homes do not grow up to be abusive.

The law defines domestic violence in very specific ways. Every state and U.S. territory has laws that allow its courts to issue protection orders, as do many Indian tribes. Each state, territory or tribe decides for itself how to define domestic violence and how its laws will help and protect victims, so the laws are different from one jurisdiction to another. Although you may be a victim of domestic violence, the laws in your jurisdiction may be written in a way that does not include or protect you. This does not mean that you are not a victim, and it does not mean that you should not seek help.

The law is a useful and important tool for increasing safety and independence, but it is not the only tool. In addition to legal assistance, you might benefit from safety planning, medical care, counseling, economic assistance and planning, job placement, childcare, eldercare or pet care assistance, or many other types of practical help and advice. You can seek assistance from advocates, shelters, support groups, the National Domestic Violence Hotline, and perhaps even your religious leader or doctor.

DOMESTIC VIOLENCE is a pattern of abusive behavior which keeps one partner in a position of power over the other partner through the use of fear, intimidation and control.

PHYSICAL ABUSE: Grabbing, pinching, shoving, slapping, hitting, hair pulling, biting, etc. Denying medical care or forcing alcohol and/ or drug use.

SEXUAL ABUSE: Coercing or attempting to coerce any sexual contact without consent, e.g., marital rape, forcing sex after physical beating, attacks on sexual parts of the body or treating another in a sexually demeaning manner.

ECONOMIC ABUSE: Making or attempting to make a person financially dependent, e.g., maintaining total control over financial resources, withholding access to money, forbidding attendance at school or employment.

EMOTIONAL ABUSE: Undermining a person's sense of self-worth, e.g., constant criticism, belittling one's abilities, name calling, damaging a partner's relationship with the children.

PSYCHOLOGICAL ABUSE: Causing fear by intimidation, threatening physical harm to self, partner or children, destruction of pets and property, mind games or forcing isolation from friends, family, school and/or work.

LEGAL ABUSE: The abuser may drag the victim into court and lie about the victim's behavior to exert control over the relationship, sometimes filing false charges. The legal battle may be over child custody or who is really the abuser in the relationship. Threats t take the children away or gain full custody by lying in court are often used by an abusing parent against the aren't who is the victim of abuse.

STALKING: In addition, stalking is often included among the types of Intimate Partner Violence. Stalking generally refers to repeated behavior that causes victims to feel a high level of fear.

Healthcare providers professionals are in a unique position to call attention to cases of domestic violence and recommend various strategies that can help both victims and abusers create safer and healthier lives for themselves.

In order to discuss domestic violence appropriately with patients and offer the m choices between healthy living and a lifetime of abuse, clinicians must know the signs of intimate partner abuse, the reasons domestic violence occurs, and the treatments available for both victims and abusers.

What is emotional abuse or verbal abuse of a spouse or intimate partner?

Mental, psychological, or emotional abuse can be verbal or nonverbal. Verbal or nonverbal abuse of a spouse or intimate partner consists of more subtle actions or behaviors than physical abuse. While physical abuse might seem worse, the scars of verbal and emotional abuse are deep. Studies show that verbal or nonverbal abuse can be much more emotionally damaging than physical abuse.

Verbal or nonverbal abuse of a spouse or intimate partner may include:

- Threatening or intimidating to gain compliance.
- Destruction of the victim's personal property and possessions, or threats to do so.
- Violence to an animal or object (such as a wall or piece of furniture) in the presence of their partner, as a way of instilling fear.
- Yelling, screaming, name-calling.
- Shaming, mocking, or criticizing the victim, either alone or in front of others.
- Possessiveness, isolation from friends and family.
- Blaming the victim for how the abuser acts or feels.
- Telling the victim that they are worthless on their own.
- Making the victim feel that there is no way out of the relationship.

What is sexual abuse or sexual exploitation of a spouse or intimate partner?

Sexual abuse often is linked to physical abuse. According to the National Coalition Against Domestic Violence, abusers who are physically violent toward their intimate partners are often sexually violent as well. Furthermore, women who are both physically and sexually abused are at a higher risk of being seriously injured or killed. Sexual abuse includes:

- **Sexual assault** – Forcing someone to participate in unwanted, unsafe, or degrading sexual activity.
- **Sexual harassment** – Using unwanted sexual advances to gain power over someone.
- **Sexual exploitation** – Examples include forcing someone to look at pornography or participate in pornographic filmmaking.

What is Stalking?

According to the <u>Office for Victims of Crime</u>, stalking is "virtually any unwanted contact between two people that directly or indirectly communicates a threat or places the victim in fear." Stalking of an intimate partner can take place *during* the relationship—with intense monitoring of the partner's activities—or after a break-up. The stalker may be trying to get their partner back, or they may wish to harm their ex as punishment for their departure.

Stalkers employ a number of threatening tactics, including:
- Making repeated phone calls, sometimes with hang-ups.
- Following and tracking the victim (possibly even with a global positioning device).
- Sending unwanted packages, cards, gifts, or letters.
- Monitoring the victim's phone calls or computer use.
- Watching the victim with hidden cameras.
- Contacting friends, family, co-workers, or neighbors for information about the victim.
- Using public records, online searching, or paid investigators to find their victim.
- Threatening to hurt the victim or their family, friends, or pets.
- Going through the victim's possessions or garbage.
- Damaging the victim's home, car, or other property.

Cyberstalking
Cyberstalking is the use of the Internet or email to stalk another person. Cyberstalking may be an additional form of stalking, or it may be the only method the abuser employs. Cyberstalking is deliberate, persistent, and personal. A cyberstalker methodically finds and contacts the victim, leaving messages that may be disturbing and inappropriate. The more you protest or respond, the more rewarded the cyberstalker feels.

The best response to cyberstalking is to ignore all attempts at communication. However, cyberstalking can progress to in-person stalking and physical violence, so you must treat it seriously and protect yourself. To learn more, read Get Help on Cyberstalking.

Stalking is unpredictable and should always be considered dangerous. Stalking can end in violence whether or not the stalker threatens to harm you. This can happen even if the stalker has no history of violence. Additionally, female stalkers are just as likely to become violent as are male stalkers. Those around the stalking victim are also in danger of being hurt. For instance, a parent, spouse, or bodyguard who makes the stalking victim unattainable may be hurt or killed as the stalker pursues the object of his or her obsession.

Seek help immediately if someone is tracking you, contacting you when you do not wish to have contact, or frightening you. For advice on dealing with a stalker and protecting yourself, read If You're Being Stalked and What to Do if You Become a Stalking Victim.

What is economic or financial abuse of a spouse or domestic partner?

Economic or financial abuse includes:
- Withholding economic resources such as money or credit cards.
- Stealing from or defrauding a partner of money or assets.
- Exploiting the intimate partner's resources for personal gain.
- Withholding physical resources such as food, clothes, necessary medications, or shelter.

- Preventing the spouse or intimate partner from working or choosing an occupation.

What is spiritual abuse of a spouse or intimate partner?

Spiritual abuse includes:
- Using the spouse's or intimate partner's religious or spiritual beliefs to manipulate them.
- Preventing the partner from practicing their religious or spiritual beliefs.
- Ridiculing the other person's religious or spiritual beliefs.
- Forcing the children to be reared in a faith that the partner has not agreed to

How do I know if I am in an abusive relationship?

There are many signs of an abusive relationship. The primary sign is fear of your partner. Other signs include a partner who belittles you or tries to control you, and feelings of self-loathing, numbness, helplessness, and desperation.

To determine whether or not you're in an abusive relationship, answer the questions in the table below. The more questions to which you answer "*yes,*" the more likely your relationship is abusive.

SIGNS OF AN ABUSIVE RELATIONSHIP

Your Inner Feelings and Thoughts

Do you :
- fear your partner a large percentage of the time?
- avoid certain topics out of fear of angering your partner?
- feel that you can't do anything right for your partner?
- ever think you deserve to be physically hurt or mistreated?
- sometimes wonder if you are the one who is crazy?
- feel afraid that your partner may try to hurt or kill you?
- feel afraid that your partner will try to take your children away?

- feel emotionally numb or helpless?
- think that domestic violence seem normal to you?

Your Partner's Violent Or Threatening Behavior

Has your partner ever:
- had a bad and unpredictable temper?
- hurt you, or threatened to hurt or kill you?
- threatened to take your children away, especially if you try to leave?
- threatened to commit suicide, especially as a way of keeping you from leaving?
- forced you to have sex when you didn't want to?
- destroyed your belongings or household objects?

Your Partner's Controlling Behavior

Does your partner:
- try to keep you from seeing your friends or family?
- make you embarrassed to invite friends or family over to your house?
- limit your access to money, the telephone, or the car?
- act excessively jealous and possessive?
- try to stop you from going where you want to go or doing what you want to do?
- check up on you, including where you've been or who you've been with?

Your Partner's Belittlement Of You

Does your partner:
- verbally abuse you?
- humiliate or criticize you in front of others?
- often ignore you or put down your opinions or contributions?
- blame you for their own violent behavior?
- objectify and disrespect those of your gender?
- see you as property or a sex object, rather than as a person?

What are the warning signs that a co-worker is a victim of domestic violence?

Domestic violence often plays out in the workplace. For instance, a husband, wife, girlfriend, or boyfriend might make threatening phone calls to their intimate partner or ex-partner. Or the worker may show injuries from physical abuse at home. If you witness a cluster of the following warning signs in a co-worker, you can reasonably suspect domestic abuse:

- Bruises and other signs of impact on the skin, with the excuse of "accidents."
- Depression, crying.
- Frequent and sudden absences.
- Frequent lateness.
- Frequent, harassing phone calls to the person while they are at work.
- Fear of the partner, references to the partner's anger.
- Decreased productivity and attentiveness.
- Isolation from friends and family.
- Insufficient resources to live (money, credit cards, car).

If you recognize signs of domestic abuse in a co-worker, talk to your Human Resources department. The Human Resources staff should be able to help the victim without your further involvement.

What are the causes of domestic abuse or domestic violence?

An individual who was abused as a child or exposed to domestic violence in the household while growing up is at an increased risk of becoming either an abuser or the abused in his or her adult relationships. In this way, domestic violence and abuse is transmitted from one generation to the next. This cycle of domestic violence is difficult to break because parents have presented abuse as the norm.

Other factors that can lead to domestic abuse include:

- Stress
- Economic hardship
- Depression
- Jealousy
- Mental illness
- Substance abuse

What are the effects of domestic violence or abuse?

The adverse effects of domestic violence or abuse can be very long-lasting. People who have been abused by a spouse or intimate partner often suffer from:

- Depression
- Anxiety attacks
- Low self-esteem
- Lack of trust in others
- Feelings of abandonment
- Anger
- Sensitivity to rejection
- Chronic health problems
- Sleeping problems
- Inability to work
- Poor relationships
- Substance abuse\

In addition to these problems, physical abuse may result in serious injury or death if the victim does not leave the relationship.

What is the effect of domestic violence on children?

Children who witness domestic violence may develop serious emotional, behavioral, developmental, or academic problems. As children, they may become violent themselves, or withdraw. Some act out at home or school; others try to be the perfect child. Children from violent homes may become depressed and have low self-esteem. As they develop, children and teens who grow up with domestic violence in the household are more likely to:

- Exhibit violent and aggressive behavior.
- Attempt suicide.
- Use and abuse drugs.
- Commit crimes, especially sexual assault.
- Become abusers in their own relationships later in life.

THE VICTIM
Why Doesn't S/he Just Leave?

Most victims do not think of themselves as battered or abused. They hope that the abuses are isolated incidents. The victim believes that if s/he is "good" the abuser will not abuse her/him. S/he thinks that then the relationship will become healthy. The abuse continues and with each episode, the victim's sense of self-esteem is chipped away—piece by piece. Ultimately s/he has no sense of self and believes the derogatory comments the abuser tells her. She feels that things are hopeless. She feels very weak and the decision to leave feels overwhelming.

They have been discussed as being similar to laboratory animals who have lost the ability to escape from painful situations who have been repeatedly shocked. They have lost their ability to escape. Passivity and non-responsiveness takes over—a learned helplessness.

How Can S/he Escape?
Often families and friends blame the victim—not wanting to hear anymore about the abuse, not wanting to take responsibility for helping him or her out of the situation.

The greatest support for victims often comes from shelters, private therapists trained in domestic violence, or acquaintances who were abused but have left the violent relationship. Victims who had emotionally supportive friends were more likely to access resources in the community for domestic violence.

Leaving the violent relationship des nit necessarily mean that the victim is safe. In fact, the US Department of Justice reports that more women are murdered when they leave abusive relationships than when they stay. Many victims leave several times and then return before they are able to make a permanent break in the relationship.

After leaving the relationship, victims have a very realistic fear of poverty. Victims in an abusive relationship often were isolated from families and not permitted to hold down a job. So their skills have become outdated and if there are young children involved, they feel unable to return to work. Women who leave an abusive relationship as is any woman obtaining a divorce will usually experience a dramatic decline in their socio-economic status. Also, the victim worries about what will happen to the children.

Even if the victim goes to a shelter, the space is only available for a limited time. Thus, victims will need to have some sort of financial resource to draw upon.

THE VICTIMZER

Abuse cuts across racial, gender, sexual orientation, educational, and socio-economic lines. Although most abusers are male, women may also be abusers. Abusers use abuse to control their partners and often deny the seriousness of their violent behavior.

- Batterers or abusers may share all or some of the following 22 characteristics:
- Externalize problems
- Demonstrate jealousy
- Use aggressive words and behavior
- Minimize and or deny and or tell frequent lies
- Impulsivity
- Show self-depreciation
- Make suicidal gestures
- Diagnosed with depression, bi-polar or other mod disorders
- Inability to Interact intimately with others on a consistent basis
- Use unusual amounts of controlling behaviors
- Resolve problems physically
- Cannot empathize with others
- Make unrealistic demands
- Compulsive use of alcohol or other drugs
- Demonstrate a lack of interpersonal and coping skills
- Manipulative
- Demonstrates socio-phobic behavior
- Exhibit contempt for women
- Show compulsive reference to sexuality
- Defy limits
- Have past history of violence
- Have low tolerance for stress

Other forces may contribute to violent behavior. Abusers may have grown up in a climate of abuse. If a person is raised with emotional, physical, verbal, and/or sexual abuse, children are at a high risk for abusing others or being abused as a n adult. Many children who have been raised in abusive homes learn that the way to survive is by using physical force.

Most abusers came from a background where some form of verbal, emotional, or physical abuse took place. There are always exceptions but sons exposed to violence toward their mothers are 1000 times more likely to become abusers in adulthood.

Abusers live in a world of denial—denying the abuse they do. They create rationalizations for their actions by putting the blame on the victim and minimizing or justifying the violence.

Some signs that may help the health care professional to identify an abuser:

- The patient's partner does the talking and answers questions for the partner.
- The patient does not make eye contact with his or her partner or cowers in his or her presence.
- The patient's partner refuses to leave the patient alone with the health care professional.
- The partner blames, belittles, or in other ways demeans his/her partner.
- The partner becomes agitated or aggressive with the professional.

THE CHILDREN

Every child in an abusive situation suffers emotional damage as a result of the violence. Each child in a violent home is a victim. They learn from observation that violence is a way of life. They are learning to be the abuser, the victim, or both The damage may be easy to see in the child who is aggressive, less so in the quiet passive child.

Research indicates that a child's exposure to a father abusing the mother is the strongest risk factor for transmitting violent behavior from one generation to the next.

Fifty per cent of the men who abused their wives also abused their children.

Many children exposed to chronic violence and abuse in the family experience post traumatic stress disorder.

Some symptoms are:
- Agitation
- Irritability
- Anger
- Mistrust
- Paranoia
- Gastrointestinal
- Nightmares
- Reenacting violence in play short attention span
- Lack of concentration
- Depression
- Aggression toward other children
- Sexual acting out
- Suicidal tendencies
- Fearfulness
- Behavioral problems in school
- Substance abuse

NOTES

AM I BEING ABUSED? CHECKLIST

(provided by <u>National Coalition Against Domestic Violence</u>)

Look over the following questions. Think about how you are being treated and how you treat your partner. Remember, when one person scares, hurts or continually puts down the other person, it's abuse.

Does your partner...

____ Embarrass or make fun of you in front of your friends or family?

____ Put down your accomplishments or goals?

____ Make you feel like you are unable to make decisions?

____ Use intimidation or threats to gain compliance?

____ Tell you that you are nothing without them?

____ Treat you roughly - grab, push, pinch, shove or hit you?

____ Call you several times a night or show up to make sure you are where you said you would be?

____ Use drugs or alcohol as an excuse for saying hurtful things or abusing you?

____ Blame you for how they feel or act?

____ Pressure you sexually for things you aren't ready for?

____ Make you feel like there "is no way out" of the relationship?

____ Prevent you from doing things you want - like spending time with your friends or family?

____ Try to keep you from leaving after a fight or leave you somewhere after a fight to "teach you a lesson"?

Do you...

____ Sometimes feel scared of how your partner will act?

____ Constantly make excuses to other people for your partner's behavior?

____ Believe that you can help your partner change if only you changed something about yourself?

____ Try not to do anything that would cause conflict or make your partner angry?

____ Always do what your partner wants you to do instead of what you want?

____ Stay with you partner because you are afraid of what your partner would do if you broke-up?

If any of these are happening in your relationship, talk to someone. Without some help, the abuse will continue.

(Adapted from Reading and Teaching Teens to Stop Violence, Nebraska Domestic Violence and Sexual Assault Coalition, Lincoln, NE).

Domestic Violence
As you can see, domestic violence is a pattern of violent behaviors, which may include physical, sexual and psychological attacks as well as economic coercion that are used against intimate partners.

The Family Violence Prevention Fund (FVPF) estimates that between 960,000 and 3.9 million incidents of violence against a current or former spouse, boyfriend or girlfriend occur annually in the USA.

Definitive numbers don't exist due to the numerous complications, including the reluctance to report on the part of many of the victims.

A recent survey by Center for Disease Control and Prevention states that about 25% of women say they have been raped and/or physically abused by a current or former spouse, live in partner, or date at some point in their lives.

While women are less likely than men to be victims of violent crime overall, women are five to eight times more likely than men to be victimized by an intimate partner. Domestic violence tends to be repetitive –about 1 in 5 women report that they had been abused more than once. They reported that they had been assaulted at least three times in the prior six months.

The level of injury resulting from physical abuse is severe. The survey concluded that 41.5% of women were injured in their prior assault, compared with 19.9% of the men. Thirty seven per cent of women who sought treatment in emergency rooms for violence-related injuries in 1994 were injured by a current or former spouse, boyfriend or girlfriend.

In 1996, approximately 1,800 murders were attributed to intimates, and nearly three out of four of these was a female victim.

The Physical Side of Violence
In addition to the obvious injuries sustained during the violence, abuse victims are more likely to experience other physical symptoms such as, heart disease, asthma, diabetes, ob-gyn complications, dental problems.

There is also an increased incidence of arthritis, chronic neck or back pain, headaches, stammering, vision problems, sexual transmitted infections, stomach ulcers, spastic colon, and frequent indigestion, diarrhea r constipation.

There are also psychological effects on the victims. Some include:

- 56% of female domestic violence victims are diagnosed with a psychiatric disorder.
- 29% of all women who attempt suicide were battered.
- About 40% of battered women have symptoms of depression anxiety or PTSD.
- Children who witness domestic violence are more likely to exhibit depression.
- Children of domestic violence are at a greater risk for abusing drugs and alcohol, becoming runaways and engaging on prostitution or sexual assaults.

The good news is that when victims seek help, their health improves dramatically.

And when abusers take responsibility for their actions and seriously address the problem, there is a high success rate in stopping future violence.

Dealing with aggressors is a complicated matter. There are some who feel that couples therapy and/or anger management classes are not appropriate modalities. Others feel that working with some types of aggressors/batterers can be effective.

THE CYCLE OF VIOLENCE

Domestic violence occurs in a cycles. There is the tension building phase in which the nonviolent partner notices growing hostility and aggression on the part of the violent partner. Nonviolent partners often describe this phase as "a time to walk on egg shells." They can sense the tension building but are not able to stop the escalation that leads to violence. The next phase is the actual violent event. This can be any behavior ranging from threatening, hitting, pinching or pushing to use of more physical force or the use of weapons. Finally, the last phase of the cycle is the make up phase or the apology phase. During this phase, the violent partner apologizes for violent or threatening behavior, promises that it will never happen again, agrees to counseling and makes a variety of other promise in an attempt to be forgiven. All phases of this cycle of violence is about the violent partner controlling or coercing the nonviolent partner.

To sum it up:

1. **The tension builds.** Mild abuse ensues. The victim starts trying to placate the abuser, by anticipating the abuser's mood in order to keep him/her from becoming upset. The victim does not realize that the violence and emotional attacks often occur because of the abuser's own internal anger and emotional issues.
2. **Significant abuse occurs.** This abuse may be physical, verbal, emotional, and/or sexual. When it begins, the victim cannot gauge how severe the abuse will be.
3. **The reconciliation begins.** The abuser is remorseful, apologizes, ad claims the abuse will stop. He/she may blame the victim and/ or deny carrying out the abuse. Both parties attempt to repair the emotional damage that has occurred.
4. **The calm before the storm.** No abuse takes place and the victim slips into a hopeful state. The victim does everything she can to keep the peaceful stage from ending. She/he goes into denial and pretends violence is a thing of the past.

The length and intensity of each phase can last from hours to months. The abuse needs to intensify on frequency and intensity over time. At some point the calm and reconciliation may not occur.

When there is no longer any loving or contrite stage in the cycle of violence, the victim may be in great danger. The abuse has reached a crisis point.

The Cycle of Non Violence

The next sections explain anger's warning signals. They familiarize you with **Anger's Warning Signals,** your external triggers, your sensations, your feelings, and your outer expressions as you get angry.

One technique for dealing with anger at this point is to use the **color meter** on the next page. Using your visual imagery you can try to go from orange (which is approaching the danger zone (red) and move yourself to yellow which is less angry, heading toward green, which is calm. Again as with the other exercises that you will learn about in subsequent chapters, the earlier you notice the early warning signs that your anger is rising, the easier it is to control and stop.

NOTES

The next section, **Controlling Behavior Checklist**, looks at the types of behaviors that you do that are controlling for other people. It will help you understand the physical, psychological and sexual abuse that you may do that is attempting to bring you power and control over another person.

NOTES

Because we take a multi-pronged approach to anger management, we examine beliefs also. Beliefs and thoughts cause you to think in a certain way and then you will experience events based on those thoughts. So as you can see from the next chart, **Beliefs That Ease Anger,** there are beliefs that you can hold that will increase anger and beliefs that you can hold that will decrease anger. As you examine the beliefs that can ease your anger, try to experience the calming feelings you would have with column two.

NOTES

Coaching Boys into Men: Taking Care of Our Sons

What you Can Do

The boys in your life need your time and energy. Your son, grandson, nephew, younger brother. The boys you teach, coach and mentor. All need you to help them grow into healthy young men.

Boys are swamped with influences outside of the home – from friends, the neighborhood, television, the internet, music, the movies… everything they see around them. They hear all kinds of messages about what it means to "be a man" – that they have to be tough and in control. There are numerous conflicting and some harmful messages being given to boys about what constitutes "being a man" in a relationship.

Boys need your advice on how to behave toward girls. Boys are watching how you and other men relate to women to figure out their own stance towards girls. So teach boys early, and teach them often, that there is no place for violence in a relationship.

Here's How:

Teach Early. It's never too soon to talk to a child about violence. Let him know how you think he should express his anger and frustration – and what is out of bounds. Talk with him about what it means to be fair, share and treat others with respect.

Be there. If it comes down to one thing you can do, this is it. Just being with boys is crucial. The time doesn't have to be spent in activities. Boys will probably not say this directly -- but they want a male presence around them, even if few words are exchanged.

Listen. Hear what he has to say. Listen to how he and his friends talk about girls. Ask him if he's ever seen abusive behavior in his friends. Is he worried about any of his friends who are being hurt in their relationships? Are any of his friends hurting anyone else?

Tell Him How. Teach him ways to express his anger without using violence. When he gets mad, tell him he can walk it out, talk it out, or take a time out. Let him know he can always come to you if he feels like things are getting out of hand. Try to give him examples of what you might say or do in situations that could turn violent.

Bring it up. A kid will never approach you and ask for guidance on how to treat women. But that doesn't mean he doesn't need it. Try watching TV with him or listening to his music. If you see or hear things that depict violence against women, tell him what you think about it. Never hesitate to let him know you don't approve of sports figures that demean women, or jokes, video games and song lyrics that do the same. And when it comes time for dating, be sure he knows that treating girls with respect is important.

Be a Role Model. Fathers, coaches and any man who spends time with boys or teens will have the greatest impact when they "walk the walk." They will learn what respect means by observing how you treat other people. So make respect a permanent way of dealing with people – when you're driving in traffic, talking with customer service reps, in restaurants with waiters, and with your family around the dinner table. He's watching what you say and do and takes his cues from you, both good and bad. Be aware of how you express your anger. Let him know how you define a healthy relationship and always treat women and girls in a way that your son can admire.

Teach Often. Your job isn't done once you get the first talk out of the way. Help him work through problems in relationships as they arise. Let him know he can come back and talk to you again anytime. Use every opportunity to reinforce the message that violence has no place in a relationship.

From:
http://endabuse.org/programs/display.php3?DocID=9916&gclid=CIS0traI4o0CFQVxHgodHDx_sg

New York State Coalition Against Domestic Violence
79 Central Avenue
Albany, NY 12206
800-942-6906
518-432-4864
Fax: 518-463-3155

MODULE VI

GAINING CONTROL OVER YOUR ANGER

GAINING CONTROL OVER YOUR ANGER

As we said earlier, our approach to managing your anger is a four-pronged approach. Throughout this book, we look at gaining control over your physiology, your cognitions, your feelings and your behavior.

So, first we will explore some cognitions that many people have about anger.

MYTHS ABOUT ANGER

Myth Number 1
Anger is inherited.
This myth assumes that anger is inherited and that it cannot be changed. Research indicates otherwise. The research findings indicate that people are not born expressing anger in one way or another; but rather, that they learn how to express their anger and more appropriate ways of expressing anger can also be learned.

Myth Number 2.
Anger automatically leads to aggression.
There are other more constructive ways to express anger. Effective anger management techniques can involve learning to express anger in assertive ways rather than aggressive ways. In this way anger can be prevented from escalating. Other skills include challenging irrational beliefs, changing negative and hostile "self talk" into more positive modes of expression, and employing a host of behavioral strategies and skills. These will be discussed later.

Myth Number 3.
You must be aggressive to get what you want.
If I don't get angry, and behave aggressively, people will think they can walk all over me.
It is easy to confuse aggression and assertiveness. Assertiveness is learning to express yourself in a non-blaming way that is respectful of the other

person. Aggressiveness is dominating, intimidating, harmful, and can cause injury to another person. Assertiveness minimizes personal harm. These skills are discussed in a later section.

Myth Number 4.
It is healthy to vent and express your anger.
Only by expressing my anger will I feel better. We should not keep anger bottled up.

Hitting something like a pillow will help me feel better with my anger. This is a common belief; however, research evidence has shown otherwise. People who vent their anger get good at venting their anger. Venting anger in an aggressive way reinforces venting anger in an aggressive way.

Myth Number 5.
Emotions are things over which I have no control.
I can't help it if other people, or situations, make me angry.
This is the greatest myth of all. This is stating that all our anger is the result of something other than us. Something other than us is the cause for our discomfort. As long as we say that someone is making us angry, then the other person is in control of our emotions. As long as we believe that other persons make us angry, they are in control over your emotions.

The idea that we can choose our emotions in any given situation sounds strange to us. Throughout our lives we have been taught that emotions are things that just happen to us and therefore are beyond our control. This is not the case. Emotions are the byproducts of what we are thinking in specific situations. If we can control our thinking, we can then control our emotions. And to control our emotions is to regain our emotional life.

Before the above discussion, did you believe any of these myths about anger to be true? Which ones?

_____

_____

_____

_____

_____

Now, after the discussion, have you changed your mind? About which myths?

_____

_____

_____

_____

_____

How Can You Begin To Alter Angry Feelings?

To repress anger or ignore the angry feelings is unhealthy. To express it impulsively will likely have negative consequences. If you hold your feelings in, they are likely to explode much like a pressure cooker.

To alter angry responses, it is important to learn where they came from—what is underneath the anger? That is why you examined the preceding ideas and behaviors to your anger response.

Usually the feelings underlying anger cause people to feel vulnerable and weak; while angry feelings help people feel, for the moment, powerful, strong and in control.

Another way to gaining control over anger is to gain control over stress. Stress and anger go hand in hand. As stress increases so too does your irritability and agitation ratings. This makes it more likely that someone will bother you and that you will lash out at them.

It therefore makes sense to learn techniques that will reduce your stress.

Getting More Cognitive....

Below are some Helpful Suggestions that are more cognitively based. Remember our thoughts cause us to define situations in certain ways, which then cause us to have certain feelings, and based on those feelings we then behave. Behavior has consequences. If the consequences are positive, we continue to define the situation, think and behave in the same way. If the consequences are negative, we would tend not to define the situation or think in the same way and we would tend to not do the behavior again.

Event Occurs-❐ We Define the Situation -❐ Leads to Thoughts -❐ Leads to Feelings -❐ Behavior-❐ Consequences-❐ Affects How We Define the Situation

So how we define a situation cause us to have certain thoughts. Based on our thoughts, we then experience certain feelings.

Thought stopping is one technique that will nip our angry definitions and thoughts in the proverbial bud.

Thought Stopping

Thought Stopping is a method that you can use to control your thoughts, which in turn will control your feelings and behavior and thus your anger response. In this method, you simply tell yourself through a series of self-comments to stop thinking the thoughts you are thinking that make you angry. In your mind, you can say, "STOP!" whenever an anger provoking thought enters your mind. Or you can say, "Don't go there. It will only upset you."

Make a list of some thought stopping sentences you can tell yourself when you begin to get angry.

_____

_____

_____

_____

_____

Sometimes people simply have not thought about beliefs that can fuel their anger. For example, if we feel that many of the negative things that happen to us happen because of something someone else did, then we are victims to other people—targets for other people to do something to. However, if we take personal responsibility for our actions, then we will not be victims. All of these premises will assist us in gaining control over ourselves.

The Principle of Personal Responsibility

This principle can help you control your anger. Basically it says that you can control your own destiny. While you cannot control the behavior of others, you can control yourself. This principle refers to taking control of your own behavior and thoughts so that you realize that what happens to you happens because of your personal choices.

- You are responsible for your own pain. You are also responsible for your own happiness.
- If your life is not going the way you want, make different choices. Start doing things differently. Change things. Take charge of what happens to you. You are the one who must change your own coping strategies to better meet your needs.

Steps to Taking Responsibility:
Develop more effective strategies for reinforcing others.
If you develop ways of reinforcing others, it starts a positive loop whereby people will then start reinforcing you.

Take care of your want or need yourself.
Take charge of your life choices. If you have a need to be on time and the person you drive with is late many times, tell them you will drive by yourself and then do it.

Develop new sources of support, and appreciation for yourself.
Do not keep doing the same thing over and over again trying to get different results. If something that you are doing is not working, do something different….so that the outcomes are different.

Set Limits. The art of saying no.
Sometimes others can be very demanding. If you continually do things that people want you to do and you do not want to o them, you will feel guilty, resentful and angry. It is not that people ask you to do things. The problem is that you have to set limits on yourself if you don't want to do something. Learn that you don't have to obey someone's commands or demands. Say no.

Negotiate Assertively.
Directly ask for what you want. Do not beat around the bush.

Let Go.
You can either accept the situation as it is or take personal responsibility for changing it.

Once you accept personal responsibility for your actions, you are never a victim.

Get Yourself A Coping Mantra

A coping mantra is anything you say to yourself that delays your anger response.

For young children, a good mantra is, "Stop, Drop, and Count to Ten." They will say this over and over in their mind and when they feel angry, they call it forth. It slows down the anger response. Some adults use this also.

A professional soccer player was prone to anger with other players on the field. His friend told him, "Keep your eye on the money" meaning that a major reason he was playing soccer was for the money and if he kept getting into squabbles or fights with his team mates, he could be thrown off the team. Every time the player started to get angry, he would touch his eye to remind himself why he was doing what he was doing and why he should keep his anger under control.

A mantra can be a word, a gesture anything that slows down the anger response.

What are some coping mantras you can employ to slow your anger response down?

_____

_____

_____

_____

_____

Work On Your Belief System

Remember the thoughts we give ourselves lead to how we feel and how we feel leads to our behavior. If we define situations are being problematic (for example, there we go again. I'm being taken advantage of because so and so isn't doing his job), then we are likely to fuel our anger thoughts. We will feel bitter and at some point we might have an angry attack.

So working on establishing positive cognitions and getting rid of negative ones will help us be more of a determining factor in our own lives.

Get Rid of "Shoulds."

"Shoulds" and "should nots" come from internalized parents. Shoulds are standards for behavior that you have internalized from your parents and from society. However they tend to be someone else's internalized standards. Shoulds and should nots make you feel guilty and resentful. Get rid of them.

List the shoulds and should nots that you have in your belief system:

_____
_____
_____
_____
_____
_____
_____

Help With Getting Rid of Shoulds

Develop Empathy for Others.

Empathy is feeling what others feel. It helps to dissipate your angry response. If you have a true understanding of the other person's point of view, it is more difficult to get angry at him or her than if you impute negative motivations to them. If you give the person negative motivations for why they are doing something that reflects back to you, it is much easier to get angry at them.

There are some techniques you can use to help you develop your empathy response.

- Put yourself in the shoes of the other person.
- Ask yourself, why are they acting this way?
- What is it in their history that is influencing their behavior (hurts, loses, pain, etc).?
- What values or beliefs are they operating under that are creating this behavior in them?
- What limitations do they have that is making them act this way (health problems, intellectual capacity, fears, lack of skills)?

Is there a person in your life that you generally impute negative motivations to? How do you do this and how can you be more empathic to this person.

_____

_____

_____

_____

_____

_____

_____

Work on Your Fallacies
Fallacies are false beliefs that we have internalized throughout life. There are some fallacies that are common to everyone and some that are unique to us as a person. Get rid of them. They only hurt you.

The Entitlement Fallacy

The entitlement fallacy is often part of our core belief system. It is based on the belief that because I want something very much, I should have it. And further, you should give it to me. As you can see, the entitlement fallacy holds quite a few assumptions:

I want something. Therefore I should have it.
You should give it to me.

So there is a demand and a should involved in the entitlement fallacy.

Make a list of your entitlement fallacies that are part of your belief system:

_____

_____

_____

_____

_____

_____

_____

Some thoughts that will help with getting rid of the entitlement fallacy:
- I can want something, but that doesn't mean someone has to give it to me.
- I can set limits on myself and others can set limits on themselves as well.
- I have the right to say no, and so do others.
- Because I have a wish, it doesn't mean others have to gratify that wish.

The Fairness Fallacy

This fairness fallacy assumes that there is some absolute standard for behavior and also that you know this standard. It assumes that when you decide that others are not following this standard, you can point it out to them and they should alter their behavior. As long as you hold on to this fallacy, you will be disappointed in the behavior of others. Get rid of it.

First of all, it is a completely subjective (based on what YOU believe to be fair and not fair).

Second it assumes that others hold the same standard (which they don't), that further they will adhere to the same standard (which they won't) and that if you point the standard out to them, that they will alter their behavior (which they won't).

Make a list of your fairness assumptions that are part of your belief system:

_____

_____

_____

_____

_____

_____

_____

When you get rid of this fallacy, you can then negotiate as peers who have competing wants and values. It is only when you accept that others have their own reality, standards and values that you can negotiate as peers and resolve issues.

Some thoughts that will help with the fairness fallacy:
- We all have different definitions of the situation.
- All persons wants and needs are equally important.
- Each want and need is legitimate and we can negotiate as peers rather than as one being "in charge" of the standard.

The Change Fallacy

Another fallacy is the Change Fallacy. This fallacy is based on the belief that you can change others if you want to and that others should change as a result of your wanting them to.

It assumes that you have control over other people, when in fact you only have control over yourself. Expecting people to change as a result of you wanting them to is a mistake. Get rid of the change fallacy as part of your belief system.

Make a list of some of the times when you expected others to change because you wanted them to:

_____

_____

_____

_____

_____

_____

Some thoughts that will help you with the change fallacy:
- People change only when they want to.
- I change only when I want to.
- People have to be ready to change.
- I have to be ready to change.

The Distributive Justice Fallacy

This fallacy is based on the premise that if people do wrongdoings they should be punished for their behavior. And that if someone hurts you, they should be punished. In fact, you should tell them the evilness of their behavior. And they should "pay" for the wrongdoing or pain they have caused you. Get rid of this fallacy. It is also based on the premise that if you do good, you should rewarded for your behavior. Doesn't work.

Make a list of all your beliefs that fit into this category:

_____

_____

_____

_____

_____

_____

_____

Some thoughts that will help you with the distributive justice fallacy:

- Anger won't get me what I want.
- The best way to get what I want is to say what I want assertively. If the person decides to give me what I ask for, then it is their choice. If they don't, then I will have to either satisfy my own want, or decide on another way or plan to get what I want.

Holding on to the above cognitive beliefs will only serve to make you feel like you are a victim in this world. It will also serve to agitate you when you expect people to behave in certain ways and they don't. And it will only fuel your anger when what you want is important to you.

Summary Pointers

Be specific in stating your needs, not global.

Do not blame other people.

Punishment, spitefulness and revenge
will not get you what you want.

Examine your assumptions.

You and only you are responsible for getting what you want
and fulfilling your needs.

Recognize that people do the best they can,
given their capabilities and their level of awareness.

Learn that you and others do what is reinforcing.
If a behavior is defined as reinforcing by a person,
a person is likely to do it again.

Some Behavioral Changes to Control Your Anger That You Can Make:

Make a 24-Hour Commitment To Act Calm

This is not a commitment to be calm; it is rather a commitment to act calm. Effective anger management starts with a specific commitment. This will help you commit to yourself and the people in your life that you will behave in a calm, non-aggressive way. Not forever. Not for a month. Not for a week. Just for 24 hours.

This will help you make it work:
Tell people your plan. Tell them that you are committed to acting calmly between _____ and _____. Absolutely—for the entire 24 hours. You will be calm. No exceptions. Not even one. 24 hours of calm behavior.

Ask for help. This might not be easy for you to do—to act calmly for 24 hours, so ask for help. Give family and friends a non-verbal signal (pulling on their ears, touching their noses) that they could do if you are looking or sounding angry.

Write down what they will do ahead of time.

Whenever you see someone making the signal, stop talking until you appear calm. Remember you don't have to be calm—just act and look calm.

Sign a 24-hour contract. Have one close person sign also as a witness.

Twenty-Four Hour Contract To Remain Calm

I,_____, between _____o'clock
on _____ and _____
o'clock on _____ promise to behave in a
calm, non-aggressive way. I will act calmly no matter what stress or
provocation may occur.

_____(Your Signature)

_____(Witness Signature)

See the benefit of getting rid of your anger attacks. Getting rid of your
anger attacks is only beneficial to you. It will improve your relationships
at work, your friendships and with those you love.

Time Out
Time out is perhaps the most useful strategy that you can incorporate
into your behaviors. This will keep your anger from escalating. It is used
successfully in many different situations and can help you slow down
your anger response or delay it completely. And anything that delays
the anger response is a good thing.

Anger is not something that happens in a flash. Even people who say
they are quick to anger have early warning signs. Your prior exercises
should have now made you aware that there are many preceding events
to your anger response.

People who do anger go through progressive steps. Beginning with
irritation, anger is kindled, and the body begins to tense. Destructive
self-statements fan the flames so to speak. And then trigger behaviors
ignite and the person is in the midst of a full-blown anger attack.

The anger attack sequence is NOT inevitable. You can stop it at any
time. Time out is one way to stop it.

When you do time out, make the T sign. Do not say anything to the other person. Do not say, "I am getting angry." Do not say anything. Just make the T sign and leave.

If the other person is your significant other, arrange ahead of time that if you start to get angry that you will be making the T sign and leaving so he or she understands.

Then, leave the premises. Go someplace for about an hour. That should be enough to cool things down.

It is important then to come back. When you come back, you should utilize the communication techniques that are listed in this book. The techniques will keep anger from escalating.

While you are gone…

It is good to do some physical exercise. Run around the block a few times. If angry thoughts come into your head, experience them and then let them go. Do NOT fuel them.

Do NOT hang on to the angry thoughts or try to build a case when you are supposed to be cooling down.

When you get back, check in with your significant other. See if they are ready to talk, again follow the communication techniques outlined in this book on P.

Practice time outs when you are not angry. If you practice when you are not angry, you will more than likely use them when you are. The purpose of time outs is to cool off and to build trust in the relationship.

If you are serious about changing your anger patterns, you can make an anger contract with your partner.

TIME OUT CONTRACT

When I realize that my or my partner's anger is escalating, I will give a T sign for a time out. I will then leave at once. I will not hit or kick anything. I will simply leave. I will not slam the door.

I will return in one hour. I will take a walk or go for a run. I will focus on calming down and not fueling my anger. During this time, I will not drink or use any drugs.

When I return, I will check in with my spouse and say, I would like to have a conversation with you. I will then communicate with him or her using the techniques on P. outlined in this book.

If my partner gives the T sign and leaves, I will not stop my partner. I will return the sign and let my partner go without any hassles, regardless of what is going on. I will not drink or take any drugs while my partner is away. I will not focus on fueling my anger.

When my partner returns, I will use the communication techniques on P. of this manual.

Signed Name_____   Date_____

Signed Name_____   Date_____

More Things To Help You Relax

Just Do It!
- Take a walk, play at the beach, work in the yard, shoot some hoops.
- Go for a jog.
- Swim a few laps.
- Roll your shoulders, raise them to your ears.
- Play relaxing music.

Get Away From It All.
Either do this in your mind or in reality. Sit in a quiet place, relax your body, and picture yourself on an island beach, floating on a cloud, walking though the woods. Focus on the details of your scene. Try to use all your senses. Smell the ocean water. Feel the sand running through your fingers. Hear the ocean waves, etc. Do this for about 20 minutes. When you open your eyes, you will feel very refreshed and relaxed.

Try to schedule times when you can really get away from it all. A couple hours over dinner, an overnight in the city, an overnight at your favorite hotel—anything that will remove you from the everyday.

Repeat To Yourself...
I am relaxed and calm.
My hands are heavy and warm.
My heartbeat is slow and regular.
I feel peaceful and still.

General Coping Thoughts List
Take a deep breath and relax.
Getting upset won't help
Just as long as I keep my cool, I'm in control.
Easy does it—there's nothing to be gained in getting mad.
I'm not going to let him or her get to me.

I can't change him/her with anger. I'll just upset myself.
I can find a way to say what I want without anger.
Stay calm—no sarcasm, no attacks.
I can stay calm and relaxed.
Relax and let go. There's no need to get my bowels in an uproar.
No one is right, no one is wrong. We just have different needs.
Stay cool, make no judgments.
No matter what is said, I know I am a good person.
I'll stay rational—anger won't solve anything.
Let them look all foolish and upset. I can stay cool and calm.
His/her opinion isn't important. I won't be pushed into losing my cool.
Bottom line, I'm in control. I'm out of here rather than say or do something dumb.
Take a time-out. Cool off, then come back and deal with it.
Some situations don't have good solutions. Looks like this is one of them. No use getting all bent out of shape about it.
It's just a hassle! Nothing more, nothing less. I can cope with hassles.
Break it down. Anger often comes from lumping things together.
Good. I'm getting better at this anger management stuff.
I got angry, but kept the lid on saying dumb things. That's progress.
It's just not worth it to get so angry.
Anger means it's time to relax and cope.
I can manage this; I'm in control.
If they want me to get angry, I'm going to disappoint them.
I can't expect people to act the way I want them to.
I don't have to take this so seriously.

Make a Coping Plan

This exercise will help you to develop a plan to an anger-provoking situation. First identify the situation. Include enough details so you are clear about the situation. Then identify one or more cues that remind you of your coping plan. Now, under when to cope, write down the behavioral red flags that tell you its time to deal with your anger. Finally under how to cope, write down the specific thoughts you plan to use.

Situation

Cues To Cope _____

When To Cope _____

How To Cope _____

Additional Information To Help With Your Anger

Act the Opposite

One of the easiest ways to change a feeling is to act the opposite.

- Smile instead of frowning. This can serve to diminish negative feelings.
- Speak softly rather than loudly. Try to Make Your Voice Soothing.
- Relax instead of tightening your muscles.
- Disengage rather than attack. Instead of attacking the other person, walk away. Make n comment. Save it for another time.
- Empathize Rather Than Judge. Say something mildly supportive, such as "This is a difficult situation for you."

To Sum Up...

- So far, you have continued to learn when you are angry. It is important to learn the early signs of when you are angry. Do you feel your anger first in the pit of your stomach? Or do you feel it first in your chest or the back of your neck. The earlier you are able to notice when you are angry, the earlier you can quench the response and keep things from escalating.
- You learned the preceding events or the triggers for your anger. You looked at core beliefs, triggering events, and impulses. You also began to learn how to control some of those impulses.
- You learned also to look at some underlying factors involved in anger. What causes you to become angry? What are your trigger buttons that get pushed? Do you feel taken advantage of? Not important enough? Not cared for? You started to see that there are important underlying triggers to your anger.
- You also started to learn to control your behavior. Once you learn what triggers your anger, and it is early on in terms of your anger response, you can learn techniques for controlling

your behavior. You can think and decide how you are going to react or behave.

You are starting to learn how to control your anger rather than allowing it to control you.

In the next section, you will learn how to communicate your feelings—your true feelings—verbally instead of physically. You will also learn techniques that will keep your arguments from escalating.

****

Anger Management

One day the wife and I were discussing anger management
And I asked her, "When I get mad at you, you never fight back.

How do you control your anger?"

She said, "I clean the toilet bowl."

I asked, "How does that help?"

She said, "I use your toothbrush"

MODULE VII

MAKING YOUR ANGER
WORK FOR YOU

LEARNING HOW TO COMMUNICATE

A step to getting rid of anger involves learning how to communicate. If we verbally learn how to eliminate distorted communicate from how we relate and if we then incorporate good communication skills into our behavioral repertoire, we are light years ahead of where we started in our goal to manage our anger.

RECOGNIZING HOW YOU DISTORT ANGER

1. Blaming:
This is probably the most destructive anger distortion. When you blame others you are assuming that they are doing bad things to you….on purpose. The next step in your thinking is probably something like, "They aren't going to get away with it!" Blaming others can help you feel better sometimes but it also is making you feel vulnerable and helpless because you are giving up the power to change the situation that is giving you pain. When you blame you are waiting for others to change their behavior. AND they never do.

Examples of Blaming:

- *We could be having a nice time if you weren't constantly nagging.*
- *If you weren't so negative, I would not feel so down in the dumps.*
- *If you would have helped me with my lesson plan, I would not have gotten such a poor evaluation from the principle.*
- *We agreed that we would car pool and then you are never on time, making me late all the time.*

What are the different ways that you blame? Give examples.

_____

_____

_____

_____

_____

_____

Instead of blaming, what could you do?

_____

_____

_____

_____

_____

2. Catastrophizing/Magnifying the Situation:

This is not just exaggerating or making a mountain out of a molehill. This is taking something bad and running with it.—taking the situation to the worst possible conclusion. By magnifying events to this degree you set yourself up to feel things based not on reality but based on your magnification of that reality.

Examples of Catastrophizing/Magnifying:

- *Because of you, my presentation is totally screwed up and I'm going to lose my job.*
- *Because of your disgusting habits, no one will socialize with us anymore. We have no friends and no one likes us.*
- *How could this have happened to me? It is the worst possible thing! I cannot come out of my house. I am so embarrassed.*
- *How could you have come home late today when we were supposed to go out? I can't believe you did this! I cannot take anymore of this. This relationship is OVER!*

What are the different ways you catastrophize or magnify? Give examples.

_____

_____

_____

_____

_____

_____

Instead of catastrophizing, what can you do?

_____

_____

_____

_____

_____

_____

3. Using Global Language:
Global language is not a good communication method in general and when the person is angry, it is only intensified. Global labels globally define the person or situation. In general they involve words like always, never, forever, etc. These are not good words to use because there are generally exceptions to everything. When applied to anger, the person usually makes global statements about a person's personality makeup.

Examples of Global Statements:

- *You are a complete loser!*
- *Is there never a time when you are not being a bitch?*
- *What a jerk. He doesn't know anything.*
- *That guy is a complete wimp. I have never seen him stand up for himself.*

What are the different ways you use global language? Use examples.

_____

_____

_____

_____

_____

_____

Instead of using global language, what can you do?

_____

_____

_____

_____

_____

_____

4. Mind reading:

This is about jumping to conclusions and attributing motivations to others based on your own definitions. Here you will assume that you know the person's "real" motives. And then you focus on that one explanation, to the exclusion of others including what they say their reasons are.

Examples of Mind reading:

- *That isn't what you meant when you said that! Don't try to play innocent with me.*
- *You did that on purpose just to aggravate me, didn't you?*
- *Look at the assignment the professor gave me. I knew he didn't like me!*
- *That isn't why you did that! You did it to make me jealous!*

What are some of the ways you do mind reading? Give examples.

_____

_____

_____

_____

_____

_____

Instead of mind reading, what can you do?

_____

_____

_____

_____

_____

_____

5. Overgeneralizations:

Overgeneralizations are exaggerations that use global terms. Using overgeneralizations, the problem is made to look bigger or worse. By exaggerating, you go way beyond the truth of the situation. You take an occasional event and make it something that occurs "all the time." Global words are always, nobody, everybody, never, etc.

Examples of Overgeneralization:

- You never help me with the kids. I do everything myself!
- No one does their job at work. Everything falls on my shoulders.
- You are never on time. We are always late for everything.
- I have to work and take care of the house. You never lift a finger to help!

What are some of the ways you over generalize? Give examples.

_____

_____

_____

_____

_____

_____

Instead of over generalizing, what can you do?

_____

_____

_____

_____

_____

_____

6. Using Shoulds:

This is when you come from a righteous position. You have right on your side. So your communication involves telling people (or demanding) what to do based on what "should" be done. Here your belief system is raised to a set of moral dictates where you have right on your side and you feel you are in a position to dictate it to everyone else.

Examples of Using Shoulds:

- Why did you do that? You should not have. It was absolutely wrong!
- That isn't fair! You should not have punished her!
- You should have known better.
- This is the right way to do it. Any other way is wrong.

What are some of the ways you use "shoulds" or should nots?"

_____

_____

_____

_____

_____

_____

Instead of using shoulds, what can you do?

_____

_____

_____

_____

_____

_____

Learn to recognize the following phrases and understand that they are not "clean" ways to communicate.

Phrases For Miscommunication:

Ordering
You must, You have to, You will…

Threatening
If you don't, then, You'd better or else…

Preaching
You should, You ought, It's your duty…

Lecturing
Here is where you're wrong, Do you realize…

Giving Answers
What I would do is, It would be best if…

Judging
You are argumentative, You'll never change…

Excusing
It's not so bad, You'll feel better…

Diagnosing
You're just trying to get attention, What you need is…

Interrogation
When? How? What? Where? Who?

Labeling
You're being unrealistic, emotional, angry…

Manipulating
Don't you think you should

The above types of beliefs will just get you into trouble and if you continue to use them will invariably lead to an anger attack. So do NOT do them. They are not good methods of communication.

Then, What Are Good Methods of Communication?

Learn these following concepts:

Use "I" statements.
Try not to use the word "you" in your conversations. When you use the word you, you are talking about the other person and not yourself. If you are irritated, using the word you generally means you are pointing a finger at the other person. YOU are always late! The only response a person can do in this situation is to defend themselves ("What do you mean? I have been on time the past 6 times.") or attack ("I'm late. What about you? You're the one who is always late.") These are guaranteed ways of making anger escalate. Remove the word you from your vocabulary.

Instead use I statements. Talk about yourself. You will not get into trouble talking about yourself. AND more importantly, the anger cycle will not escalate.

Stay Focused.
Do not bring up the kitchen sink. Stay focused on the one annoyance.

Communicate in the Here and Now. No History.
Stay in the here and now. Do not bring up events from the year of the flood.

A very long time ago, when people went food shopping, they were given trading stamps for their purchases. These trading stamps could be traded in for household items. The more trading stamps, the bigger the prize. Just like people used to save up trading stamps, so too do some individuals save up small annoyances, small feelings of anger, threat, anxiety to later cash them in for some larger feeling. The result is usually a major battle.

If the small feeling or annoyance were communicated when it happened, the result would have been resolution and thereby closure and elimination of the negative feeling.

Do Not Attack. Solve the Problem.
Do not go for the jugular. Stay away from calling names. If there is a problem, stay on the problem and use problem solving techniques on P. Try to move right into problem solving techniques. It will keep arguments from escalating.

Learn How to Mirror.
Mirroring is one of the most important techniques you will learn in terms of keeping your anger in check. Mirroring involves allowing people to feel heard and it prevents the argument/discussion from escalating. Mirroring involves paraphrasing what your partner has said. It means that you will repeat what they have just verbalized. If you use mirroring, anger will not escalate. Also your partner will feel heard. Using an I statement and talking about yourself in the here and now will effectively communicate what you want and if your partner mirrors you, you both will stay out of trouble. "I get upset when I am late for events." And then your partner can mirror you, "So…what you're saying is, "You get upset when you are late for things." This type of statement will keep things calm.

Validate.
Validation does not indicate agreement. It indicates understanding. Validating is a cognitive function. Basically it says I understand where you are coming from. Again, it doesn't mean that you agree, it just means you understand.

Empathize.

Empathizing with someone means that you can feel what they are feeling—that if you put yourself in their shoes, you would be able to feel their sadness, their pain or their joy. It means that you can be sad for their pain. Whereas validation is cognitive (in the head), empathy is from the heart.

The following is a typical communication technique that is used with couples but it can be applied to any relationship where there is a frustration or annoyance. It is an extremely effective method of communication and will serve to keep any argument from escalating.

Communication Method

Person A	**Person B**
Say your frustration using I statements	Partner mirrors
Say how you feel around the frustration (leaving out the you)	Partner mirrors
Validates and Empathizes Ask for three behavior changes around this frustration	Partner mirrors
	Partner chooses one
Then shake hands; you have a deal.	

Example

Person A	**Person B**
I am upset because we will be late	You are upset because we will be late
When I am late, I feel insecure and anxious	When you are late, you feel insecure and anxious
	I can understand why you want to be on time.
	You must worry every time we go someplace that I will late to pick you up.

Yes and I would like:

For you not be late on Mondays	You would like be to be on time on Mondays
For you to be on time when we have a party	You would like me to be on time when we have a party
And for you to call when you're going to be late	And for me to call if I'm going to be late
	I choose number 2—I will be on time when we have a party

As you can see, the communication went full circle. It started out with the frustration, moved to the feeling associated with the frustration and then moved into behavioral change requests.

The couple could also go into the feelings in more depth and perhaps person A could connect the feeling of insecurity and anxiety when late to a feeling from childhood. But the point is that if communication stuck to these few rules, anger would NOT escalate and problems would be solved.

Another method for communication that will serve to solve the problem and not cause anger to escalate is problem solving. Below are some steps that you can take that will help you solve some of the problems you will encounter in life.

PROBLEM SOLVING

Problem solving involves a series of steps that can be carried out consciously and intentionally.

Step 1. Define the Problem.

What is wrong? What do I want to change? This is the first step in the problem solving process and perhaps the most important. Be specific about the problem. It is called operationalizing. When you operationalize the problem, you get very specific, very concrete and the problem becomes measurable. For example, if a person says their problem is that they are not happy, it is very difficult to deal with the entire realm of unhappiness. However, if you ask the person, what specific things are they doing when they are happy and they reply, reading—well reading is something you can see and you can measure. Define the problem in terms of minute detail. Try to use very precise language, taking into account everyone's opinion.

Step 2. Brainstorm Solutions.

Take a piece of paper and start brainstorming any possible solutions, no matter how silly they sound. Write them down. Be as creative as you want and try not to judge what you are writing. When you brainstorm:

Be uncritical.
Be wild and crazy.
Be prolific.
Be Creative.

Step 3. Evaluate Solutions and Analyze the Potential Consequences.

Look at each solutions and try to predict what the outcome would be for each solution. Carefully think about each one. You can even write out a list of pros and cons for each one. You can then give each pro and each con a number based on how important the item is to you. Then you can add up the numbers to see if the pros outweigh the cons or visa versa.

Step 4. Choose a Solution and Then Try It Out.

Choose one solution and create a plan to try it out. This is after you have weighed the possible pros, cons and outcomes of the solution. Remember this is only ONE of your potential solutions and you are ONLY testing it. If you try it and are not satisfied, you have many more solutions that you can try.

Take a deep breath and just DO IT!.

Step 5. Evaluate the Outcome. If Necessary, Try Another Solution.

Once you have tried your first solution, you can evaluate how well it met your original goals. Did you accomplish what you wanted? Beware of some of the traps of what you did. Do not blame yourself if it did not work. Try to remain calm, and try not to evaluate success as all or none.

Psychological Growth Record:

It is also helpful to keep a record of your growth regarding your anger. Make copies of the Change Form and regularly update. In this way you can see where you've been and where you are heading. It helps you make a plan of action—to implement your desires for change into an action plan for change.

In the left hand column, write down the changes you see yourself making. In the right hand column, write down the specific steps or behaviors that you are taking to accomplish those changes.

CHANGE FORM

Changes I am Making	Specific Steps

PRACTICE WHAT YOU PREACH

Next are a series of vignettes describing situations that may or may not elicit or trigger your anger. These are real stories of real clients. All names have been changed and in some cases, the story has been somewhat altered to protect the client.

To prepare, first go to your comfortable chair and do your breathing exercises, your visual imagery or your muscle relaxation exercises to put yourself in a deep state of muscle relaxation. Once you are in a deep state of muscle relaxation, imagine yourself in the following situations.

Barry was arguing with his girlfriend when he left her apartment on Sunday evening. He thought she had lied to him about getting a call from her ex-boyfriend. So Barry left thinking he didn't "need to put up with her crap.". As he was walking home, a car sped by him, startling him. He became so angry he picked up a bottle lying on the floor and threw it at the car, smashing the back window where young children were sitting in the back seat. Barry was arrested and while on parole is to attend 10 sessions of anger management workshop.

What do you make of this? As you were reading the vignette, did you notice any changes in yourself—in your physiology, in your breathing? Did you feel your anger starting to rise up at all? If you were in Barry's shoes, how would you have handled it. How could you have avoided the situation entirely?

_____

_____

_____

_____

_____

_____

_____

What steps could you have taken if you were Barry to quell your anger?

_____

_____

_____

_____

_____

_____

_____

_____

Keith and his girlfriend would frequently party together and then get into heated arguments. This is exactly what happened last Saturday night. Keith tried to walk away from her this time so he left her at the party and returned to his dorm room. However, she wanted to continue the argument and followed him to his dorm. He let her in after she repeatedly banged on the door. The argument escalated and he tried to leave the room. She blocked the door with her body and he "lost it." He tried to pull her out of the way, and tried to shove her past the door. When that didn't work, he pulled her hair to move her out of the way. The police were called and he was charged with domestic violence and sentenced to attend anger management classes.

What do you make of this? As you were reading the vignette, did you notice any changes in yourself—in your physiology, in your breathing? Did you feel your anger starting to rise up or not? If you were in Keith's shoes, how would you have handled it. How could have avoided the situation entirely?

_____

_____

_____

_____

_____

_____

_____

What steps would you have taken if you were Keith to quell your anger?

_____

_____

_____

_____

_____

_____

_____

_____

Danny has trouble verbally expressing his needs. His stress usually builds inside of him until he explodes. Whenever he tries to express himself, his wife, his boss, his father usually take control of the conversation and then Danny withdraws. This pattern repeats itself until a time when he can no longer keep the 'lid' on his anger and he then explodes. His wife told him the marriage was over unless he went to anger management. So he did. Danny has been trying 'anger management' but has decided it's really not helping him and he wants to stop. However, he cannot discuss this in session nor call the therapist so he e mails instead.

What do you make of this? As you were reading the vignette, did you notice any changes in yourself—in your physiology, in your breathing? Did you feel your anger starting to rise up? If you were in Danny's shoes, how would you have handled it? How could you have avoided the situation entirely?

_____

_____

_____

_____

_____

_____

_____

_____

What steps would you have taken if you were Danny to quell your anger?

_____

_____

_____

_____

_____

_____

_____

_____

Concetta works as a maid in a prestigious hotel. She works very hard to help support her family. She has been working there for 15 years, often putting in extra time to help out her boss. Several new women have been hired recently and Concetta feels they are getting the easier jobs and not working as much as she is. She decided to take a day off after seeing the new girls calling in sick and taking time off. When she approached the boss, he said no. Concetta became very angry and started screaming in his office. The boss said she had to attend anger management or she would be fired.

What do you make of this? As you were reading the vignette, did you notice any changes in yourself—in your physiology, in your breathing? Did you feel your anger starting to rise up? If you were in Concetta's 's shoes, how would you have handled it.? How could Concetta have avoided the situation entirely?

_____

_____

_____

_____

_____

_____

_____

_____

What steps could you have taken if you were Concetta to quell your anger?

_____

_____

_____

_____

_____

_____

_____

Next, remember the situation, the exact event that brought you to anger management classes. Try to image yourself back to that situation. Remember what happened. Remember what you did. Remember how you finally got to anger management.

Now that you have taken the classes, how do you see the situation? As you were thinking back to how angry you were then, did you notice any changes in yourself—in your physiology, in your breathing? Did you feel your anger starting to rise up again? Now how would you have handled that old situation? How could you have avoided the situation entirely?

_____

_____

_____

_____

_____

_____

_____

_____

WHAT TO DO WHEN YOU GET ANGRY

- Use your twenty-four hour commitment to stay calm.
- Use your time out procedures.
- Check out any faulty thinking that you might be doing.
- Use thought stopping techniques.
- Identify stresses in your environment and take steps to reduce them.
- Use your relaxation techniques.
- Practice your communication techniques to stay calm.
- Review your materials regularly.

What else can you do?

_____

_____

_____

_____

_____

_____

_____

_____

RELAPSE

How do think anger management should occur?
Do you think it occurs in a smooth linear way, with your anger episodes just gradually disappearing like a miracle. It doesn't. Anger Management occurs in peaks and valleys, meaning you'll go along fine for a month and then you'll say something that reminds you of how you used to act. It is important to realize that because you expressed anger, it isn't the end of the world. It is important to keep it in perspective. If you express anger once, it doesn't mean all is lost. It means you expressed anger once and you will get back on track.

How does relapse happen?
Relapse is a slow insidious process. It does not happen all at once with a major slip up. It happens slowly—almost so slowly that it goes unnoticed. We think of relapse as a slip-up, NOT as a failure. A slip-up does not mean that you are back to square one with your anger. You have learned too much for that to occur. It means you slipped-up. It is important to understand that.

are the warning signs of slipping up?
- You start to express anger in the "old ways."
- You aren't monitoring your stress level the way you used to.
- You aren't monitoring your relaxation techniques that way you used to.
- You start communicating in the "old ways."
- You put yourself in old trigger situations.

What is the process of relapse?
You start to feel a sense of self-control. This is akin to self-denial. You begin to think you are absolutely "cured," so you can skip your relaxation techniques. You are able to not monitor your cognitions. All is well so you don't have to go to therapy. You may begin to push the envelope and put yourself in anger eliciting situation. You start to feel

like you can control even the most triggering of your triggers. Therefore you take more and more risks.

What are some places, people, and things I should avoid?
- Your stressors in life--whether negative or positive.
- Don't let yourself become overwhelmed.
- Changes whether positive or negative.
- Stay away from high trigger situations—plain and simple.
- Do not fester over past hurts and lost opportunities.
- Do not isolate yourself.
- Do not ignore anger expressions.
- Do not drink or drug.
- Don't miss therapy appointments.
- Don't call in sick to work or school unless you have a fever.
- Do not withdraw from friends and family.
- Get rid of your morbid thoughts—I will be alone; I will be abandoned; Everyone hates me.

What are some places, people and things I should be doing?
- Pay attention to what other people are saying.
- Eat three meals a day.
- Keep your therapy appointments.
- Get plenty of sleep.
- Take your multi vitamin.
- Stay on top of your anger monitoring and your communication.
- Take showers every day and do some exercise.
- Work with your therapist on your high risk triggers.
- If you need help, get it. Don't wait.

**Pick Yourself Up, Dust Yourself Off,
And GET BACK ON TRACK!**

Now list some of your high trigger buttons that you think might be problematic for you?

_____

_____

_____

_____

_____

_____

_____

How are you going to deal with each trigger event?

_____

_____

_____

_____

_____

_____

_____

All the major religions hold forgiveness as a very important concept. Some believe forgiveness is important for the evolutions of society; others believe forgiveness is necessary to do good will to others.

The Budhists have another interpretation. For them forgiveness is seen as a practice to prevent harmful emotions from causing havoc on one's mental well-being. Buddhism recognizes that feelings of hatred and ill-will leave a lasting effect on our mind karma and instead encourages the cultivation of emotions which leave a wholesome effect. "In contemplating the law of karma, we realize that it is not a matter of seeking revenge but of practicing metta and forgiveness, for the victimizer is, truly, the most unfortunate of all.
(From Wikipedia)

Regarding anger management, forgiveness is the step that puts closure on the anger events. If you can forgive your trigger person, then he or she is no longer a trigger person. They have lost their hold on you. Have you thought about doing this?

Could you write down your thoughts about this.

_____

_____

_____

_____

_____

_____

_____

Could you write down some words or a letter to the person you were most angry at?

_____

_____

_____

_____

_____

_____

_____

Can you forgive them? Write some thoughts or a letter to them.

_____

_____

_____

_____

_____

_____

_____

One of the most important elements in this program is for you to be able to forgive yourself. Do you think you are able to forgive yourself. Could you write down your thoughts about this.

_____
_____
_____
_____
_____
_____
_____

Can you write a letter of forgiveness to yourself?

_____
_____
_____
_____
_____
_____
_____

Forgiveness does not change the past, but it does enlarge the future.
Paul Boese

MODULE VIII

GROUP DYNAMICS

HISTORY OF GROUP THERAPY

1900-1920: The Practical Beginnings

- **Joseph Gaither Pratt** studied how people with medical issues (Tuberculosis) fared and coped when grouped together.

- **L. Cody Marsh** developed a group treatment for a psychiatric population.

- **Edward Lazell** (1919) introduced group therapy with schizophrenics.

1920-1930- Theoretical Underpinnings

- **Gustave Le Bon** published *The Crowd*. This generated much interest in how individuals behaved in groups.

- **Sigmund Freud** published *Group Psychology and the Analysis of the Ego.*

- **Burrow** developed a program in NYC that enabled individuals to free themselves from their masks.

- **Jacob L. Moreno** introduced the name **Group Therapy.**

1930s-1945 The Age of Integration

- **Louis Wender** conducted the first psychoanalytic group in NY.

- **Samuel Richard Slavson** worked with children in groups.

- In 1943 Slavson founded **the American Group Therapy Association.**

- **Alexander Wolff** said group therapy was cost effective for those who cannot afford individual psychoanalysis.

- **Wolf and Schwartz** started the first **Group Therapy Certificate** program in New York Medical College in the late 1940s.

- **Moreno** felt psychoanalysis dwelled too much on the past and he started the **American Society Psychotherapy of Psychodrama**. He started a debate between the analysts and the more here and now focused Moreno. Moreno felt he was the **Father of Group Therapy** not Pratt and he coined the term **Group Psychotherapy.**

1945-1960 The Age of Expansion

WWI created an interest in group therapy. WWII prompted the growth of group therapy. Theorists dealt with the overflow of troops in hospitals.

- **Wilfred Bion** looked at the unconscious life of the group, using Melanie Klein 's Object Relations Theory.

- **Henry Ezriel** acted Bion's unconscious life of the group but also believed the therapist must also pay attention to individual dynamics.

- **S.H. Foulkes** termed the leader of the group is the conductor who is non-authoritarion and non-directive, who attends to both group and individuals.

- **Kurt Lewin** developed a meta-theory of group life. **Lewin's Field Theory** became the basis for the T Group movement in Britain and US. The group possesses qualities that transcend those of any individuals.

1960-1970 Group Therapy Enters the Community

The Community Mental Health Act of 1963 prompted the widespread use of the group.

- **Carl Rogers** devised the basic encounter group in the 1960s.

1970-1985

- **Irving Yalom** published *The Theory and Practice of Group Psychotherapy* in 1970, the bible of group therapy. He believed the purpose of the group is to enable the individual to improve his or her capacity to have positive relationships with others.

1985-Present

Managed Health Care influences all of therapy.
Addressed the following:

- Increasing cost of Mental Health Therapy
- Need for short term mental health care
- Need for clear treatment plans
- Need for more collaborative model between different types of practitioners
- Increasing importance of the professional organizations in the field,
- An increasing attention to ethical and legal rights
- The focus on addressing multiculturalism and diversity

Dr. Joan D. Atwood

Five Stages of Group Development

Successful groups move through five phases throughout their lifetime. Tuckman identifies five stages of development and calls them: Forming, Storming, Norming, Performing, Adjourning.

Other researchers have labeled similar stages of group development. Charrier (1974) calls them Polite or Why We're Here, Bid for Power, Constructive, and Esprit. Cooke and Widdis (1988) call them Polite or Purpose, Power, Positive, and Proficient.

Jones (1974) depicts the model to show the four typical stages in the evolution of a group in relation to two major dimensions of personal relations and task functions.

The personal relations dimension of the model encompasses all the interrelationships that people develop and sustain in the group – their feelings, expectations, commitments, assumptions, and problems with one another. The stages of personal relations correlate with the development of the identity and functions of a group from the personal orientations of individual members. The stages of task functions correlate with the progress of a group in understanding and accomplishing its work. As a group moves through the personal relations and task functions stages simultaneously, the progress and setbacks in one dimension influence the behavior and progress in the other.

Task Functions
The stages of group development are sequential and developmental. A group will proceed through these five stages only as far as its members are willing to grow. Group cohesiveness seems to depend on how well group members can relate in the same phase at the same time. Each member must be prepared to give up something at each step in order to make the group move to the next stage. The timing of each will depend on the nature of the group, the members, and the leadership of the group. Issues and concerns must be resolved in each stage before

the group can move on. If the group is not able to resolve such issues, the dominant behavior will become either apathy or conflict, and group disintegration will result.

Stage 1: Forming

When you are in the stage for forming or formation, your personal relationships are categorized as dependent. The members are the groups need a safe environment, and therefore find themselves dependent on group leaders for guidance and direction. Members of the groups have a desire for acceptance by the group and a need to be sure that the group is safe. They want to avoid conflict. Serious issues and feelings are avoided, and people focus on being busy with routines, such as when they will meet, etc. They set about gathering impressions and data about the similarities and differences among them and forming preferences for future sub-grouping. Rules of behavior seem to be to keep things simple and avoid controversy. Serious topics and feelings are avoided. This is a comfortable stage to be in but nothing much is getting done.

The major task functions also concern orientation. Members attempt to become oriented to the task as well as to one another. Discussion centers around defining the scope of the task, how to approach it, and similar concerns.

To grow from this stage to the next, each member must relinquish the comfort of non-threatening topics and risk the possibility of conflict.

This is the stage of joining, welcoming, building relationships.

If the purpose or membership seems exclusive, or people don't feel welcomed, they might not join or might be tentative or suspicious.

Appropriate Leadership Style

Since groups in this phase require definitions of their roles and goals they will need information from the leader about the group's agenda, deadlines, etc. The leader should provide as much structure as possible and become the emotional center of the team.

Specific Leader Actions
You should listen carefully, be visible, maintain open communication/ feedback channels for the team, offer support and reassurance, keep group members accountable for day-to-day results, and create team traditions.

Specific Group Member Responsibilities
Group members can help the team building process by accepting the new team identity, by learning the group's mission, and by getting to know one another.

Stage 2: Storming
In group settings, conflict is inevitable in personal relationships of group members, particularly since everyone organizes, has different feelings, ideas, attitude and beliefs. Because of fear of exposure or weakness weakness and even failing at tasks, individuals may want a concrete structure or clarification and commitment to this structure placed.

Although these conflicts may or may not be vocalized, these issues do exists. Delegating roles, such as who will be responsible for what part, what the guidelines and how to evaluate, as well as who leadership will be, how structure is set, who has what power will reflect in conflicts.

Some members may become more vocal than others who remain silent. This may be because of the discomfort created at this stage, and there may be an imminent shift in behaviors based on emerging issues of competition and hostility.

To combat these kinds of conflicts and move to the next stage, creating a testing and proving mentality to a problem solving mentality is crucial. To do so, the most important trait in helping these groups is to listen to them.

This is the stage of setting expectations, establishing styles, learning leadership and member roles, establishing processes and establishing goals.

If expectations are not clear, people may not meet them.

If expectations are not met, frustrations may arise.

If judgments arise about styles and roles, people may act critically.

If oppressive behavior happens and or is condoned, people may be hurt or want apologies or even want to quit.

If the group's goals don't match the members' goals, members may be frustrated.

At this stage leaders should be stating expectations. Individual confrontations may be happening and listening should be taking place. Group discussions are now starting.

Appropriate Leadership Style

Groups in this stage still require a high level of directive supervision, but also need considerable support. The leader must not only serve as mediator, but also as a teacher of group norms and values. The leader also needs to listen to group problems, manage conflicts, encourage participation, provide recognition, and build alliances.

Specific Leader Actions

You need to stay approachable; provide answers, answers, and more answers; repeat key information often; set short-term goals; restate mission, objectives, and priorities; and create opportunities for participation.

Specific Group Member Responsibilities

Group members must focus on the commonalties of the group and not the differences.

Stage 3: Norming

According to Tuckman's norming stage, cohesion is defined by interpersonal relations. Acknowledging who contributed what, community building and maintenance and solving issues that arise are all necessary to change preconceived notions or opinions. These can be addressed by other group members and this allows for active participation by allowing group members to question each other. This also allows for leadership to be a shared activity, and addresses to dissolve the formation of cliques. Trust and personal relations are created by allowing each other to develop personal relationships. During this stage, group cohesion is created which creates a sense of catharsis at having resolved interpersonal conflicts.

The major task function of stage three is the data flow between group members; they share feelings and ideas, solicit and give feedback to one another, and explore actions related to the task. Creativity is high. If this stage of data flow and cohesion is attained by the group members, their interactions are characterized by openness and sharing of information on both a personal and task level. They feel good about being part of an effective group.

The major drawback of the Norming stage is that members may begin to fear the inevitable future break-up of the group; they may resist change of any sort.

At this stage members will air dissatisfactions. They will start to find ways through conflict. They will assess leadership. And they will assess the member's role.

If people attack the leader or organization, the leader may be defensive and may not lead well.

If the leader doesn't deal with the conflict in the manner members want, members may feel distrust and May judge the leader.

A support the leader exercise, individual discussions and group discussions should be occurring.

Appropriate Leadership Style

Groups in this stage understand the goals and tasks more thoroughly and are willing to work hard to achieve these goals. The leader should work to make the members less dependent on his/her own leadership, but still focus on providing the support people need to mesh their activities productively.

Specific Leader Actions

You must continue to keep members focused and communication channels open, solicit participation, and encourage creative thinking. Be prepared to translate organizational goals into team goals.

Specific Group Member Responsibilities

At this point group members need to master the team skills and become interdependent by removing the leader from the center of everything.

Stage 4: Performing

Not all groups will reach stage four, which is the performing stage. If group members do find themselves at this stage, they are able to demonstrate true interdependence because of the expansion of their capacity, range and depth of personal relations. During this stage, individuals are able to function as a single unit, in smaller groups are as a whole unit with equal facility. Based on the group's needs, roles and leadership may vary. This stage is marked by interdependence in personal relations and problem solving in the realm of task functions. Productivity will be demonstrated in the highest capacity, and individuals rely on self-assurance instead of group approval. Task orientation and unity is demonstrated; group identity is complete, group moral is high, and group loyalty is intense. The groups focus on problem solving, create solutions and optimum group development. Groups will try to solve problems through experimenting and focus on achievement.

Here the group is functioning well and the group sees conflict as opportunity.

If there are unresolved issues, they will keep resurfacing in another form until resolved.

If member performance isn't supported, members may burn out or attack leadership.

If leadership isn't supported, leaders may burn out, not appreciate members, and not cultivate new leaders.

Group discussions are occurring and appreciations for members and leaders is occurring.

Appropriate Leadership Style
Groups in this phase have worked through their adjustments and have become energized by the prospect of achievement. The leader can serve as ambassador/philosopher and take a less active role by allowing the group members to run the day to day business of the group.

Specific Leader Actions
You need to provide resources, remove obstacles, reward high performance, stimulate interaction, emphasize teamwork, and celebrate successes.

Specific Group Member Responsibilities
Group members can help by taking on more of the team's business and letting the team leader operate at the boundaries of the team.

Stage 5: Adjourniing
In Tuckman's final stage, adjourning, groups will work on terminating task behaviors and disengagement from relationships. Concluding involves recognizing participation and what was achieved through these groups. Members of the group also have the opportunity to have their own personal goodbyes. What is also demonstrated by group members

is apprehension, in effect – a minor crisis. For some, the termination of the group can be a regressive moment from giving up control to give up inclusion to the group. Interventions associated with the stage can be task termination and the disengagement process.

The Concept of Development

Here it is important to put closure on tasks, put closure on relationships and prepare for the next group.

If people have unspoken feelings about closure, they may procrastinate or otherwise sabotage projects.

Leadership Style in this Model Moves From:

- **Directing**
- **Coaching**
- **Motivating**
- **Mentoring**

Applications of the Model

Facilitators must be sensitive to the needs of group members in various stages of group development. By referring to this model, a facilitator can gain some insight into the inevitable stages through which a group must pass before attaining the benefits of stage four. This insight is useful both in planning group learning situations and for monitoring a group's progress while it is in session.

As a tool to facilitate group communication and development, the model is most effective at stage three of a group's development. At this point, the members have experienced stages one and two and are in a receptive mode to internalize the implications of stage four. The model provides them with a goal they can visualize and work toward.

Paying earnest attention to strategies for reaching stage four can facilitate the movement to that stage.

If the concepts of the model are presented when a group is in stage one, they may fall on deaf ears, receiving only polite attention. If presented in stage two, the concepts become food for conflicts or are ground into oblivion by the process of organization. At stage four, the model is unnecessary.

SPECIFIC GUIDELINES AND SUGGESTIONS
FOR RUNNING GROUPS

SECTION I: Getting Ready for Group

- **Pre-group Considerations**
  - Leader should be qualified and experienced in running groups
  - What will leader's main functions be?
  - What will be the main goals of the group?
  - Where will group be held? How long will it last?
  - Is your group accessible to physically handicapped?
  - Is group sensitive to members of diversity?
  - Are your sessions set up?
  - What evaluation procedures will you use to determine the degree to which the group has met its goals?
  - What follow-up procedures will you use to help members of the group integrate what they have learned?
  - Have you a procedure for screening members?
  - Some guideline questions are:
    - Why do you want to join the group?
    - Have you ever participated in a group before?
    - Do you understand the purposes and nature of the group?
    - Do you have any fears about joining the group?
    - How ready are you to take a critical look at your self and address your anger issues?
    - What are some specific personal concerns you would like to explore?
    - What would you most hope to get from the group?
    - What would you like to know about me?

- **Preparing Parents of Minors**
  - Get written permission from parents or legal guardians before allowing members to participate in group. Make sure you know your state's requirements.
  - You can invite parents and their children and/or teens to discuss their questions or concerns. Sending letters and holding a meeting with parents can prevent many problems from arising later on.

- **Preparing Teenagers and Adults**
  - With teenagers, a letter should be sent to the parents requesting permission and a meeting should be held with both the parents and the teenagers.
  - With adults, there should be a pre-group screening to determine if the individual is appropriate for the group. See screening questions above.

- **Setting Goals**
  - Members and leaders need to set goals for themselves—both at the beginning of the group and the beginning of each session for maximum learning to occur. At the beginning of each session, a brief questionnaire can be given asking members to rate how well they are coping with the group; how well they are managing their stress; and if they feel they are making progress. The members can tell one another about their specific goals.

- **Preparing Contracts**
  - Here members write out specific behaviors that they would like to change and what they are willing to do outside of group to make these changes. Contracting is a useful method to use with psycho-educational groups. The leader and other members can say if they think the members' goals are realistic.

- **Guidelines for Designing Effective Contracts**
  - Below are some guidelines for designing effective contracts:
    - Keep the language concise and simple
    - State the goals in behavioral terms.
    - Strive for realistic and obtainable goals.
    - Identify short and long term goals.
    - Relate personal goals to the general goals and purpose of the group.

- **Reading**
  - Reading can be a good asset for psycho-educational and therapy groups.
  - Reading can be used as a focusing technique. Themes may emerge in a group and assigning reading around that theme is helpful. Taming Your Gremlin is one such assigned book.

- **Writing Journals**
  - Members can spend 10 minutes each day recording their feelings, situations, behaviors, and ideas for courses of action. Journaling provides continuity between sessions and it also helps members use session time more efficiently.
  - Some relevant questions group members can look at in-between sessions are:
    - What is it like to be in the group?
    - How do I define the people in the group? How do I see myself in the group?
    - How do I sabotage myself in the group?
    - How can I challenge myself in the group?
    - How do I avoid sharing information in the group?
    - What is happening in the group when I am comfortable in sharing?
  - Members could also write down their reactions to the group and 10 minutes before the end of each session, members can share those feelings.

- **Letter Writing**
  - Here members can write a letter to the most important person in their life. This could be a letter of apology, a letter of love. The only stipulation is that it ends on a positive note. The letter does not need to be given to the person it was written for or the member may decide to share it.

- **Giving Specific Questions**
  - Group leaders can design questions ahead of time that then are given to the group to ponder. In an adolescent group, the leader may ask:
    - How important to you is being accepted by the peer group?
    - How fearful are you of relating to members of the same sex? Of the opposite sex?
    - How much pressure do you feel to decide on a career?

- **Structured Questionnaires**
  - Here the leader may decide to put all the questions together in a questionnaire. Sentence Completion questionnaires are very helpful.
    - What I want most from this group is _____.
    - Thinking about being in this group for the next 12 weeks, I _____.
    - One personal concern I would hope to bring up is_____.
    - Something I particularly like about myself is _____.

- **Setting up a Problem Checklist**
  - Setting up a problem checklist is another way of helping members decide how they want to use group time. Or a teenage group, develop a list of problems teenagers typically experience and ask them to write down a rating in terms of how they experience each item.

- **Using Imagination**
  - Imagine you are a novel.
    - What is your title?
    - What are your chapter headings?
    - Do you deliver what you say you will deliver?
    - Which chapters were the hardest to write?
    - The easiest?
    - Will people feel you delivered what you advertised?
    - After people have read you cover to cover, what do you think they will think?

- **Handouts**
  - Handouts will assist members to get the most out of a group. If the group is a psycho-educational group, then giving members handouts on The Differences between Assertive and Aggressive Behavior would be helpful, as would a handout on Good Communication Techniques.

- **Preparing Leaders**
  - Get yourself ready:
    - How ready do I feel for this? Am I available to the members?
    - Do I want to do this Group?
    - How effective am I in my personal life?
    - Am I doing what I would hope the members would do with their lives?
    - Am I professionally confident?
    - Do I believe in the process of the group? Or am I doing the group merely because I was told to?

- **Getting Ready**
  - Relax before you go into the group.
  - Be aware f your thoughts and feelings as you approach a group session.
  - Try some of the exercises on yourself.

- Spend time with your co-leader if you have one.
- Review what you plan on doing each session and discuss this with your co-leader.
- Devote some time to thinking about the previous session.

SECTION II: The Initial Stage

- Characteristics of the Initial Stage
  - o Physical Setting and Arrangements
  - o Privacy
  - o Comfort
  - o Seating Arrangements
- Getting Groups Started
  - o Introductions
  - o Introducing Someone Else
  - o Setting a Time Limit
  - o Using Dyads and Small Groups
- The Leader's Role
  - o Focusing Members
  - o Focusing on an Issue Outside of Group
    - Techniques to Help to Focus on Issue Outside of Group
- Creating Trust
  - o Dealing with Mistrust
  - o Some Signs that Trust is Created
  - o Some Signs that Trust is Lacking
  - o Fostering Trust
- Addressing Initial Resistance
- Starting a Session
- Ending a Session
- Member Evaluations
- Leader Evaluations

SECTION III: Transition Stage

- **Dealing with Defensive and/or Problem Behaviors**
  - **Avoid labeling members as defensive or resistant.** Attempt to be patient and strive to understand what purpose their difficult behavior is serving.
    - *Have an external focus.*
      Members in this stage frequently focus on other members and on events that are external to themselves. They may blame others in or out of the group to make up for their own inability to trust. A method for dealing with this is to ask the person who is doing the blaming, "Why don't you turn toward John and tell him how his behavior is affecting you?"

    - *Using impersonal and global language.*
      If the leader asks a question about how members feel about being in an anger management group, and Jim answers, "No one wants to be in here." He is using language that will keep focus off of himself. Leader could then refocus and say, "How do you feel about being in the group, Jim?"

      Some examples:
      Member: People are cautious about opening up in here.
      Leader: What are you cautious about John?

    - *Asking questions of others.*
      A defense in the transition stage is members asking questions of others. This drains the energy of the group and the question should be refused to the individual.

    - *The person who is silent.*
      Leaders need to respect the silent member. The leader needs to create an environment that invites members to

participate rather than force them to participate. Other members will eventually ask the member to participate. Some techniques for dealing is to form an inner group of those who are participating and have them discuss what they would like to know about those who are not participating. Or to have the silent members form an inner circle and discuss how they feel about their silence.

- *The person who monopolizes.*
  Often the member who is monopolizing is not challenged by the group. In this case, sharing your reflections and observations may be all that is necessary. necessary.

- **Exploring Common Fears**
  - *I'm afraid you won't like me.*
  - *There's someone here who bothers me.*
  - *I'm afraid to look at what I am really like.*
  - *I can't see why we have to share every feeling.*
  - *We seem stuck in the group.*
  - *I don't feel safe here.*
  - *I can't identify with anyone here.*

- **Leader Issues**
  In this stage leader challenges tend to emerge. It is important to deal with these challenges in an appropriate way or it may effect the group. Some of the challenges will be based in reality. Some challenges may include:

  - *Why do we always have to focus on the negative?*
  - *Your leaders aren't sharing enough of yourselves.*
  - *Your leaders aren't very helpful.*
  - *You blew it.*

SECTION IV: The Working Stage

- **Characteristics of the Working Stage:**
  In this stage, you can link members by focusing on common themes. Generally members are eager to initiate work. There is a here and now focus in this stage. Here members talk about what they currently think and feel. They are also willing to have direct and focused interactions with each other. Members more readily identify their goals and concerns and they take responsibility for them. Group cohesion increases. Not all groups reach this stage.

- **Working with Emerging Themes**
  Some typical themes that might emerge during this stage are:

  - *I'm confused and don't know what to do.*
  - *I'm afraid to get close to people.*
  - *This isn't the real world.*
  - *I'm afraid I might never stop crying.*
  - *I'm afraid I'll lose control.*

- **Working With Intense Emotions In All Members At Once**
  - **Once this has occurred, you must make a decision as to which member to work with.**
    - *Bring the focus back to one person.*
    - *Move next to the person who is crying.*
    - *You can pair people up to work together.*

- **Working With Projections and Other Problems of Self-Awareness**
  - *I can't talk to my parents.*
  - *My father wouldn't talk in English.*
  - *Here let me help you.*
  - *A great part of me wants this, and a part of me wants that.*

- *I so much want your approval.*
- *I feel very empty.*
- *I feel unappreciated.*
- *I don't like being overweight.*
- *What I get out of that is_____.*

SECTION IV: The Final Stage

- **Tasks to Accomplish**
  - Members are encouraged to face the inevitable ending of the group and to discuss fully their feelings of separation.
  - Members are encouraged to complete any unfinished business they have with their members or the leaders
  - Members are taught how to leave the group and how to carry with them what they have learned and especially how to talk to significant people in their lives.
  - Leaders help members discover ways of creating their own support systems after they leave the group.
  - Specific plans for follow up work and evaluation are made.
  - Consideration is given to how members might discount a group experience and to teach members relapse prevention techniques.
- **Summing Up**
- **Dealing with Unfinished Work**
- **Arranging Homework Assignments**
- **Leaders Comments to Members**
- **Terminating the Group**
  - **Preparing for Termination**
    - Reviewing the highlights of the group experience.
    - Expressing unacknowledged aspects of group experience.
    - Exploring the issue of separation.
    - Rehearsing new roles.
    - Being specific about outcomes and plans.
    - Projecting the future.

- o Summarizing personal reactions to the group.
- o Making contracts
- **Continued Assessment and Follow Up**
  - Encouraging Contact with Other Group Members
  - Arranging a Follow up Session
  - Suggesting Further Work
- **Evaluating the Group**
  - Member Evaluation Form
  - Leader Evaluation Form

GUIDELINES AND SUGGESTIONS FOR GROUP MEMBERS

- *Have a focus.* When you have focus, you find yourself committing to getting something productive from the group by focusing on what it is that you hope to accomplish. This includes clarifying any goals you may have, reviewing issues that you want explored or addressed, and specific changes you want to make. You will also clarify actions you would take to make these changes and can document it if it helps.

- *Be flexible.* Although it helps to approach the group with some idea of what you want to explore, don't be so committed to your agenda that you cannot deal spontaneously within the group. Be open to pursuing alternative paths if you are affected by others in your group.

- *Don't wait to work.* It is easy to let a group session go by without getting around to what you hope to do or say. The longer you wait to involve yourself, the harder it will become. Challenge yourself to say something at the beginning of each group, even if it's a brief statement of what it was like for you to come to the group that day.

- *Be "greedy."* The success of a group depends on your being eager to do your own work. This doesn't mean that you should monopolize time or be insensitive to the difficulty others may have in getting into the spotlight. But if you constantly wait until it's your turn, or try to monitor how much of the group's time should be allotted to you, you will inhibit the spontaneity and enthusiasm that can make a group exciting and productive.

- *Pay attention to feelings.* Intellectual discussions are great, but an experiential group is also about your feelings and convictions, not just your thinking. Explore your life at an emotional level. If you start sentences with, "I think…. Or "My opinion is…., you probably aren't exploring your life on a feeling level. Be open to letting yourself experience them as soon as you are in a session. Connect group discussions to yourself personally.

- ***Express yourself.*** Most of us are in the habit of censoring our expression of thoughts and feelings. We are afraid of being inappropriate or afraid that we will magnify our feelings. These fears are not unfounded but we do worse to ourselves if we do not verbalize them. A group is an ideal place to find out what would happen if we said what was in our minds. If you have feelings that relate to the group, be willing to express them.

- ***Be an active participant.*** You will help yourself most if you participate in the group. Members who are silent observers benefit less than members who participate.

- ***Experiment.*** Look at the group as a place in which you are safer and freer to express yourself in different ways and try out different sides to you. Then you can carry these new behaviors into the outside world. Then you can report to the group how you are behaving differently outside.

- ***Be willing explore.*** No matter how well your life is going now, it can be enriched by the opportunity to explore your feelings, values, beliefs, attitudes, and thoughts and to consider changes you may want to make. Even if you do not have a pressing issue in your life, assume that the issues that come up for you are worth exploring.

- ***Don't expect change to be instantaneous.*** If you do seek change in your life, remember that such changes do not usually happen all at once or without some backsliding. Don't be overly critical of yourself if you experience setbacks. Realize that it will take time to change longstanding patterns and there might be a tendency to revert to familiar ways when you are faced with stressful, situations. Give yourself credit that you are willing to try and aim for small changes that you can see yourself making.

- **Don't expect others to appreciate your changes.** Some people in your life may have an investment in keeping you the way you are now. You may find less support for your struggles outside the group than in it. Use the group to explore ways to handle any resistance you may encounter outside. It is a good idea to remind yourself that you are in this group primarily to make all the changes you want to make in yourself, not to change someone else.

- **Don't expect to be fully understood within the group.** Groups heighten a sense of intimacy and provide opportunity for being understood by others; however, it is unlikely that you will be fully understood. Members will see certain dimensions of you but will not have a good idea of what you are like otherwise. You don't have to qualify and footnote everything you say. If you decide to explore a relationship you are in, better not to focus on giving a full detailed picture of it, you will be talking forever. Better to resign yourself in advance to the idea that others won't and can't have the full picture.

- **Don't expect to fully understand others in the group.** You do a disservice to others in the group if you suppose that you have them all figured out. Like you, they are presumably working on expressing a side of themselves that they do not have an opportunity to express. People are very complex.

- **Stick with one feeling at a time.** Try to immediately express your feeling when you feel it. Try not to censor one feeling because you are feeling a contradictory one. You may have mixed emotions about an issue, but I you fully want to face that issue, try to stick with those feelings one at a time.

- *Avoid advising, interpreting and questioning.* As you listen to others in that group, you will often be tempted to offer advice. Too much advice advice can inundate people. You are in the group to express yourself. Thepeople could begin to withdraw if they get too much advice. Express your feelings and experiences of your own that the person stimulated. Similarly, sometimes everyone takes on the role of the group leader in interpreting the speaker. Here the speaker can get defensive feeling like she is the only one working on an issue. People also get defensive when faced with an onslaught of questions. Questions can be asked that open people up rather than shut them down. If you want to ask a question, preface it by saying why you are interested. Let others know of your personal interest in hearing the answer. You can explore more if you tell them your personal reactions to the issue rather than questioning them about theirs.

- *Don't gossip.* Gossiping is talking about someone in the third person. If the person is not in the room, your group leader may encourage you to pretend that the person you want to talk about is in the room and have you speak directly to this person. This usually leads to a powerful expression of feelings and/or thoughts. Try this… "I'm angry with him because…." Then say… "I'm angry with you because…." Which do you think will elicit more emotion?

- *Don't be quick to comfort.* If you rush too quickly to soothe someone's pain, you may be curtailing their ability and desire to fully express what they want to say. People grow from living through their pain so let them do it.

- *Give feedback.* When people express something that touches you, let them know by sharing your own feelings and reactions. Even if your feedback is not easy to express and may be difficult to listen to, it can be useful if it is delivered in a caring and respectful manner. It will engender trust in the group and leads you to honesty in your daily life. Rather than telling group members how to solve their problems, tell them about your own struggle with your own problems. Emphasize feedback that will give others a clearer sense of how their behavior affects you personally. Avoid judging people, but do let them know what specific behaviors of theirs might be getting in your way in dealing with them. Also let them know which behaviors might bring them closer to you.

- *Be open to feedback.* When others give you feedback about their reactions to your work, remember that, like you, they are there to try out new ways of expressing themselves directly. The most constructive approach is to listen and to think their reactions over until you get a grasp on what parts of it fit.

- *Avoid storytelling.* If you go on at length in providing information about you, you wind up distracting everyone, including yourself. Avoid narratives of your history. Express what is present, or express what is past if you are struggling with these events.

- *Exaggerate.* You can sometimes worry too much about whether you are genuine if you focus on a feeling that you have. Rather then wonder if you are exaggerating an emotion, give yourself permission to nurture them a bit and discover where they lead. Of course, you won't want to fake it, but you may get in touch with something genuine by throwing yourself into what you feel.

- *Avoid sarcasm.* A main goal of participants is an experiential group is to learn to express feelings, including anger, in a direct manner. If you must be angry, say so directly. Do not use pot shots and sarcasm, which people don't know how to interpret. If you are hostile, which is indirect anger, not only does this negatively affect others around you but it also builds up inside you. If you learn to express even minor irritations there is a reduced risk that you will store up negative reactions that are unexpressed, which eventually lead to hostility and are expressed through sarcasm.

- *Include group leaders in your reactions.* It is normal for members to react to group leaders with feelings borrowed from the past, from fantasy, and from reality. You can turn this reaction to advantage by making it a special point to explore and express your feelings about your group leaders. Let them know how what they are saying and doing affects you.

- *Beware of labels.* Watch out for generalizations, summary statements and labels you use to describe yourself. Such self-imposed labels invite others to treat you as an outsider and insist on pigeonholing you for the duration of the group. Be ready to challenge others if you think they are reducing you to one dimension. Don't assume that labels tell you all there is to know about you or someone else.

- *Make friends with your defenses.* Your defenses have helped you get where you are today. They may need modification; come to understand your defenses by understanding how they protect you. You may sabotage your own work by saying things like I'm not smart. When you become aware of your typical patterns of avoidance, challenge these defenses and try to substitute direct and effective behavior.

- *Decide for yourself how much to disclose.* To find out about yourself, you need to take some risks by saying more than you are comfortable saying. Pushing yourself should be distinguished from disclosing things about yourself that you are doing simply because you think others expect it. Group is a good place to respect your own boundaries but it is also a place to respect them.

- *Carry your work outside the group.* You will find new ways of expressing yourself within the group. Try these behaviors out in everyday life with due respect for timing and with caution. Don't burden yourself with the expectation that you should disclose everything that you've disclosed to the group to a person in your life outside the group. You may role-play your father in the group. This does not mean that you have to role-play it with your actual father outside the group. Decide what you want to say to people outside the group. If you feel you want a closer relationship with your father, set behavioral goals for yourself outside the group that will help you get what you want.

- *Don't be stopped by setbacks.* You may have a specific vision of how you want to behave differently. But remember you may have relapses at times. Instead of getting discouraged and feeling that you will never change, be patient with temporary setbacks. Realize that you have spent years developing these patters and when you are under pressure you may revert back to them even tho they are old patterns and may not serve you well any longer.

- *Express your feelings.* Some feelings are easier to express than others. Groups usually focus on feelings that are causing members some difficulty. Try to talk about feelings that you frequently try to deny. Share not only feelings but share joys as well!

- *Think about your thinking.* Learn to monitor your self talk. Identify those beliefs that work against you. If you tell yourself that people don't like you, reflect on how easily you could be setting yourself up for defeat. You could be creating a host of self-fulfilling prophecies that keep you from feeling and acting the way you like. Once you've identified these negative patterns, bring them to a session and begin to challenge them. Learn to argue with those voices in your head that keep you from becoming the person you want to be.

- *Take responsibility for what you accomplish.* The leaders and members in your group will no doubt be interested in drawing you out. But remember that what you accomplish in the group is completely up to you. Don't wait for others to call on you. Learn to ask what you want. You will determine what and how much you get.

- *Be familiar with your culture.* Recognize that your cultural background will influence how you think and behave. Explore ways that you continue to be influenced by your background. Although there are some values that you appreciate that you have gotten from your culture, be open to questioning some of them. How would you like to modify some of them?

- *Develop a reading program.* Reading can be therapeutic and can also provide you with material that you can bring to group. Select books that will help you put your life experiences in perspective. Read books that teach you new patterns of thinking and behaving.

- *Write in your journal.* Writing in a journal will help you remember the experiences that you've had in group. If you rely on memory, chances are pretty good that you will forget. Even brief entries are helpful to monitor yourself and keep track of how well you are attaining your goals.

- *Respect confidentiality.* Keep in mind how easy it might be to betray the confidences of others. Make it a practice not to talk about group outside the group. If you talk about the group outside the group, talk about your own experiences. And what you are learning.

MODULE IX
EMOTIONAL INTELLIGENCE

EMOTIONAL INTELLIGENCE

What is Emotional Intelligence?
You've probably heard and read about Emotional Intelligence. There's a lot of information available. But what is it and where has the idea come from? Emotional Intelligence is not a fad or a passing trend but the end result of years of research into human behavior.

In the words of EI expert Daniel Goleman, Emotional Intelligence is: *The capacity for recognizing our own feelings and those of others, for motivating ourselves, for managing emotions well in ourselves and in our relationships."*

In other words, Emotional Intelligence has nothing to do with IQ, or how clever you are, but everything to do with how self-aware you are and how you interact with others. Why concern yourself with EI? Recent research has shown that EI is twice as important as IQ in determining future career success and also that people with higher levels of EI are less likely to have emotional outbursts. And the really good news is that it can be developed.

A study of Harvard graduates showed that their entrance results (their basic intelligence or IQ) had a negative or zero correlation with their future career success. Likewise, most of us have come across someone who's "lost it" in a meeting or gone blank during a presentation. Emotions that are out of control can have a massive impact on how others perceive you. "Emotions are contagious, and a single person can influence the emotional tone of a group by modeling." This is a key factor in managing one's anger. If your anger is chronic or pervasive in your life then you are infusing that emotion into all the interpersonal situations in which you participate.

Emotional Intelligence can be broken down into 2 main areas; personal competence and social competence. Personal competence involves your ability to be self aware or recognize your feelings and their impact on others. It also includes knowing your own strengths and limitations and having sense of self worth or self confidence. Personal competence includes self-management. Being able to keep destructive feelings and behaviors under control is key having a high emotional intelligence. People who have high levels of EI are able to display honesty and trustworthiness. They are able to be flexible in the face of changing situations. Another skill essential to high EI is being able to tolerate stress. You must be able to navigate stressful situations and relationships without loosing control. Reality testing is a skill that allows you to perceive what is happening around you while measuring how much is out in front of you and how much is colored by your own feelings and experiences. This is crucial to high EI. Finally, good problem solving abilities add the your measure of EI. Problem solving is about being able to identify the problem and allow yourself to be creative and open in generating solutions.

As we are social beings and therefore, live our lives in relationships with other people, social competence is also an important factor in emotional intelligence. Social competence is about how people manage their relationships. Specifically, the skills in this area relate to having empathy and being able to perceive other peoples' feelings and perspectives especially when they are different from you own.

Impact of Emotional Intelligence
So how important is EI and why should anyone invest in developing it? If you are looking to controlling your anger, then developing your EI is very important. We all knew people at school who were geniuses in the classroom. But what happened to them after school ended? How many were destined for great success?

A study of Harvard graduates showed that their entrance results (in other words, their basic intelligence, or IQ) had a negative or zero correlation with their future career success. Likewise, most of us have come across someone who's "lost it" in a meeting or gone blank during a presentation. Emotions that are out of control can have a massive impact on how others perceive you.

What area of your Emotional Intelligence would you like to work on—to develop further?

_____

_____

_____

_____

_____

_____

_____

What traits do you have regarding EI are you satisfied with?

_____

_____

_____

_____

_____

_____

_____

Utilizing the skills you learned in this program, which skills do you think would be most useful to you to improve EI??

_____

_____

_____

_____

_____

_____

_____

Learning to understand yourself, and to accurately know how others see you, by developing your EI is the key to improving your chances of success, as well as overcoming your anger outbursts. There are numerous studies to back this up, but here are a few highlights:

- Software developers with high levels of EI can develop effective software three times faster than others
- Sales consultants with high levels of EI generate twice the revenue of their colleagues
- A research project by the Hay Group providing EI development support for 45 sales people in the insurance industry demonstrated profound differences between the group receiving the EI support and a matched sample (control group) of those who did not. The goal of the project was to run the comparison between the two groups for a full calendar year, but the researchers called the program off after seven months because the difference in sales results was so large that they could not afford to wait another five months to train the control group.

For more information, see
http://www.eiconsortium.org/research/what_is_emotional_
intelligence.htm

Measurements of Emotional Intelligence

To take the Emotional Intelligence Test Online, go here: http://www.queendom.com/tests/access page/index.htm? idRegTest=1121

Additional Measures of EI:
Self-report measures of EQ
Self-report assessments of EI include the EQi, the Swinburne University Emotional Intelligence Test (SUEIT) or GENOS EI, the EQ Map, the Six Seconds Emotional Intelligence Assessment (SEI), the Schutte Self-Report Emotional Intelligence Test (SSEIT), the ECI, the Ei360, and a test by Tett, Fox, and Wang (2005). Some of these inventories, such as the Ei360, also include sections for informant-reports in order to validate the self-reported responses.

The Schutte Self-Report Emotional Intelligence Test (Schutte et al., 1998), a publicly printed behavior inventory, was one of the earliest measures to assess EI. It is one of the only inventories based on Mayer and colleagues' (1990) four-branch model, and it has been outdated by advancements in Mayer and colleagues' assessment techniques (see below) and by newer EI inventories. Although its use was relegated to basic research, it was a first of its kind.

One of the more advanced self-report measures is the Emotional Intelligence Appraisal by Bradberry and Greaves (2005c). The Emotional Intelligence Appraisal measures four skills of EI that were spelled out in Daniel Goleman's model:

- Self-Awareness
- Self-Management
- Social Awareness
- Relationship Management

Six Seconds (out of San Mateo, California) has validated the Six Seconds Emotional Intelligence Assessment (SEI). The SEI test was developed by using a model created by experts in learning and teaching EQ called the *Straightforward Model.*

Responses to the SEI are statistically reliable, and scores on the SEI predict 55% of the variance of a combination of quality of life, relationship effectiveness, health, and personal effectiveness (based on forward stepwise regression with self-reported outcomes, see the white paper. "Emotional Intelligence and Success"). Responses to the SEI can be used to create a detailed report, which is over 20 pages long, and includes at least 16 specific methods to improve EI.

Ability-based measures of EI

The Mayer-Salovey-Caruso Emotional Intelligence Test (MSCEIT) is a measure of EI involving a series of emotion-based problem solving items. Consistent with Mayer and colleagues' (1990) notion of EI as a type of *intelligence*, the test is modeled off of ability-based IQ tests. Consequently, it has high face validity in reference to some conceptions of EI but not to others.

Due to the non-objective nature of its items, correct answers on the MSCEIT have been determined by the consensus of experts and of a large standardized sample of 5000 (MacCann, Roberts, Matthews, & Zeidner, 2004; Roberts, Zeidner, & Matthews, 2001). The MSCEIT allows responses to be scored using either the experts' consensus or the large sample's (responses scored using each of these techniques will strongly correlate with each other, however both options are supplied due to theoretical disagreements about consensus based assessment).

Training in Emotional Intelligence

EI training specialists have advanced the practice of using training programs to enhance clients' EI. These programs often use pre and post-test scores in order to measure EI change. Specific EI tests that are commonly used in these programs include the SEI, the BarOn EQi, the EQ Map, the ECI, and the Ei360. Specialists (such as Freedman, Brovedani, Cannon, Darnell, Orme) have documented case studies, which show measurable differences in pre and post training EI, and have anecdotal evidence of improvement in social and emotional functioning. However, it is debatable whether EI can actually be taught or whether it is static like IQ.

Emotional Intelligence to Resolve Conflicts

An important subfield of EI explores how emotional intelligence can be applied to benefit people dealing with a conflict or negotiation issue. Researchers on emotional intelligence and conflict have examined: The effects of emotional intelligence on creating and claiming value in a negotiation (Roger Fisher and Daniel Shapiro of Harvard's Negotiation Project, Foo, Elfenbein, Tan, & Aik, 2004); the role of compassion and anger in negotiation (Allred); the effect of intelligence -- both cognitive and emotional -- upon the negotiation process (Fulmer and Barry, 2004).

20 Stumbling Blocks of Even the Most Intelligent People….

From Sternberg, R. (1986). Intelligence Applied.
New York: Harcourt Brace Jovanovich.

1. *Lack of Motivation.*
2. *Lack of Impulse Control.*
3. *Lack of Perseverance and Preservation.*
4. *Using the Wrong Abilities.*
5. *Inability to translate thought into Action.*
6. *Lack of Product Orientation.*
7. *Inability to Complete Tasks.*
8. *Failure to Initiate.*
9. *Fear of Failure.*
10. *Procrastination.*
11. *Blaming Others.*
12. *Excessive Self-Pity.*
13. *Excessive Dependency.*
14. *Wallowing in Personal Difficulties.*
15. *Distractibility and Lack of Concentration.*
16. *Spreading Oneself Too Thick or Too Thin.*
17. *Inability to Delay Gratification.*
18. *Inability to See the Forest for the Trees.*
19. *Lack of Balance Between Critical, Analytical Thinking, and Creative Synthetic Thinking.*
20. *Too Little or Too much Self-Confidence.*

Using the above list, list the traits that you feel you could work on to improve your EI.

_____

_____

_____

_____

_____

_____

_____

Using the above list, list the traits you have already incorporated.

_____

_____

_____

_____

_____

_____

_____

How do you think you incorporated those traits? What skills did you use?

_____

_____

_____

_____

_____

_____

How could you use those skills to improve the traits that you would like to improve?

_____

_____

_____

_____

_____

_____

_____

MODULE X

CLOSING EXERCISES AND GRADUATION

Inventory of Positive Traits and Experiences

What was the happiest period of your life?

_____

_____

_____

_____

_____

_____

_____

What things do you do well?

_____

_____

_____

_____

_____

_____

Tell me about a positive turning point in your life.

_____

_____

_____

_____

_____

_____

Was there any time when you exhibited great courage? If yes, tell me about it.

_____

_____

_____

_____

_____

_____

_____

What are some improvements you have made in your self since beginning module I?

_____

_____

_____

_____

_____

_____

Tell me about some (non drug related) peak experiences you have had. You currently have. You would like to have.

_____

_____

_____

_____

_____

_____

What are some things you want to do right now at this point in your life.

_____

_____

_____

_____

_____

_____

What does your family usually do on Thanksgiving?

_____

_____

_____

_____

_____

_____

_____

What do they usually do at Christmas, Chanukah, etc?

_____

_____

_____

_____

_____

_____

_____

What books have you read recently that you liked?

_____

_____

_____

_____

_____

_____

How do you plan to get involved with your Mother/Father in their old age if they are still alive?

_____

_____

_____

_____

_____

_____

_____

What are your favorite sports?

_____

_____

_____

_____

_____

_____

Do you have a hobby that you enjoy?

_____

_____

_____

_____

_____

_____

What do your friends like about you?

_____

_____

_____

_____

_____

_____

What do your parents like about you?

_____

_____

_____

_____
_____
_____

_____

What do your siblings like about you?

_____
_____
_____
_____
_____
_____

What are some things you really like about you?

_____
_____
_____
_____
_____
_____

What are some things you really believe in?

_____
_____
_____
_____
_____
_____

Where do you see yourself five years from now?

_____
_____

_____

_____

_____

_____

_____

What are some ideas you have of the good life?

_____

_____

_____

_____

_____

_____

Is there anything you would like to change about yourself? What?

_____

_____

_____

_____

_____

_____

Tell me some of the things you feel and do that make you satisfied with your life.

_____

_____

_____

_____

_____

_____

What are some of the things that you do that you are proud of?

_____

_____

_____

_____

_____

_____

What are some of the things you are really good at?

_____

_____

_____

_____

_____

_____

Describe something nice you have done for a person recently.

_____

_____

_____

_____

_____

_____

What is the best thing you have done for someone else?

_____

_____

_____

_____

_____

_____

What is the best thing you have done for yourself?

_____

_____

_____

_____

_____

_____

What have you learned about yourself from taking this personal inventory?

_____

_____

_____

_____

_____

_____

Tell me about the new you.

_____

_____

_____

_____

_____

Draw a picture of the new you.

_____

_____

_____

_____

_____

EVALUATION OF THE WORKBOOK

1. What did you like the most about the workbook?

_____

_____

_____

_____

_____

_____

_____

2. What didn't you like about the workbook?

_____

_____

_____

_____

_____

_____

3. What is the most valuable lesson you learned?

_____

_____

_____

_____

_____

_____

4. What changes have you seen in yourself?

_____

_____

_____

_____

_____

_____

5. What other topics would you have liked to learn more about?

_____

_____

_____

_____

_____

_____

6. Did you learn anything interesting about yourself that you did not learn before?

_____

_____

_____

_____

_____

_____

7. Do you think you have the skills to better control your anger and your stress?

_____

_____

_____

_____

_____

_____

Closing Exercises and Graduation

In this section you can review your anger control plans and rate the treatment components for their usefulness and familiarity. You will also complete a closing exercise and be awarded a certificate of completion.

Closing Exercise:

1. What have you learned from the anger management course?

_____

_____

_____

_____

_____

_____

_____

2. Thinking of all the information you learned while in this program, what strategies do you think will help you the most in terms of managing your anger?

_____

_____

_____

_____

_____

_____

_____

3. In what ways can you continue to improve your anger management skills? Do you feel there are any areas that still need improvement?

_____

_____

_____

_____

_____

_____

_____

NOTES

ADDITIONAL MATERIALS

Individual Intake Form

Date: _____

Name: _____

Address: _____City: _____ Zip: _____

Home Phone: _____Cell Phone: _____
Email: _____

Referred by: _____

Occupation: _____Place of Business _____

Work Address: _____

Work Phone: _____ Birth date: _____
Age: _____ Sex: _____

Is there any other person living in your household: _____ yes _____no

If yes, please give their names and their relationship to you _____
_____
_____
_____

Have you ever been married? _____yes _____no If yes, to
whom and for how long? _____

Do you have any children? _____yes _____no If yes, please list below:
_____

Counseling History

From: _____ To: _____ With Whom? _____

For What? _____

Basic Health: __good __fair __poor When was your last physical exam?
_____

Who is your Physician? _____

Are you taking any medication at this time? _____yes _____no
If yes, what? _____

Are you taking any over the counter medications, herbs, supplements, etc.? _____yes _____no If yes, what?_____

Are you taking any medications for allergies? _____yes _____no If yes, what? _____

Do you have any physical, emotional, or mental condition now or in the past that I need to be aware of? _____yes _____no If yes, what? _____

Have you ever been hospitalized? _____yes _____no If so, for what? _____

CURRENT REASON FOR SEEKING COUNSELING:

Briefly describe the problem for which you wish to have counseling?
_____
_____

What would you like to see happen as a result of counseling?
_____

The thing which concerns me the most right now is?
_____

IT IS CUSTOMARY TO PAY YOUR THERAPIST AFTER EACH SESSION.

A COUNSELING SESSION IS NORMALLY <u>50</u> MINUTES.

POLICY

A <u>24</u>-HOUR CANCELLATION NOTICE IS APPRECIATED; OTHERWISE USUAL FEE WILL BE CHARGED.

I UNDERSTAND THAT SUICIDAL THREATS, HOMICIDAL THREATS OR CHILD ABUSE BY AN ADULT TO A CHILD WILL BE REPORTED.

I UNDERSTAND AND GIVE PERMISSION TO MY THERAPIST TO SEEK CLINICAL SUPERVISION OR CONSULTATION ABOUT MY SITUATION WHEN NECESSARY.

Signature: _____

Please print name: _____

Date: _____

DUTY TO WARN

Although confidentiality and privileged communication remain rights of all clients of psychotherapists according to state law, some courts have held that if an individual intends to take harmful or dangerous action against another human being, or against himself or herself, it is the psychotherapist's duty to warn the person or the family of the person who is likely to suffer the results himself or herself.

State Laws require that all mental health professionals report incidents of any type of child abuse or neglect to appropriate agencies.

The psychotherapist will under no circumstances inform such individuals without first sharing that intention with the client. Every effort will be made to resolve the issue before such a breach of confidentiality takes place.

_____   _____

Therapist's signature   Client's Signature

No Violence Contract

Physical violence is extremely harmful to all relationships. Participation in physically aggressive behavior on the part of one or both partners results in numerous negative consequences. Some of these effects include: loss of trust, loss of respect for self and partner, emotional and physical pain, lack of intimacy, and less time spent together. Interpersonal violence greatly interferes with progress in couple therapy. In fact, interpersonal violence and couple therapy are not compatible. For these reasons, we are making a commitment, both written and verbal, to stop all violence in our relationship.

By violence, we mean harming or threatening to harm your partner either physically (e.g., pushing, shoving, restraining) or emotionally (e.g., belittling, name calling).

We can tell that we are coming close to becoming violent when…

_____

_____

_____

To help prevent violence from occurring, we will do one or more of the following to stop ourselves from escalating when we begin to see the cues listed above:

_____

_____

_____

If any of the above items occur even once, we have decided that it would be best to discontinue relationship therapy and begin individual therapy until we are able to control our physical aggression toward each other.

_____   _____

Client's signature   Date

_____   _____
Client's signature   Date

_____   _____
Therapist's signature   Date

General References

APA, Controlling Anger -- Before It Controls You, http://www.apa.org/topics/controlanger.html

Barkley, R.A. (1997). *DefiantChildren: A Clinician's Manual for Assessment and Parent Training.* 2nd ed. New York: Guilford Press.

Beck, R. and Fernnandez, E. (1998). Cognitive behavioral therapy in the treatment of anger: A meta-analysis. *Cognitive Therapy and Research*, 22, 63 – 74.

Bultler, G. and Hope, T. (2007) *Managing Your Mind: The Mental Fitness Guide*, 2nd ed. New York: Oxford University Press.

Chapman, R.A.; Shedlack, K.J.; and France, J. (2006). Stop, think, relax: An adaptive self-control training strategy for individuals with mental retardation and coexisting psychiatric illness. *Cognitive and Behavioral Practice*, 13(3), 205 – 214.

Ellis, A. (1979). Rational-emotive therapy. In: Corsini, R. (Ed.), *Current Psychotherapies* (pp. 185 – 229). Itasca, II: Peacock Publishers.

Ellis, A. (1992). Anger: How to Live With and Without It, New York:Citadel Press Book.

Falcon, C. T. (2004). Controlling Anger in Relationships, http://www.sensiblepsychology.com/improving_anger.htm

Feindler, E.L. (2006). *Anger Related Disorders: A Practitioner's Guide to Comparative Treatments* (Ed.). New York: Springer Publishing Co.

Gentry, D.W. (2000). Anger-Free: Ten Basic Steps to Managing Your Anger, Morrow, William & Co.

Gorkin, M. (08/17/00). "ALARMING "YOU'S or DISARMING "I'S: POWER STRUGGLES vs. POWERFUL STRATEGIES PART I", http://www.selfhelpmagazine.com/articles/growth/aggression. html

Gorkin, M. (1986) "Anger or Aggression: Confronting the Passionate Edge," Legal Assistant Today

Gorkin, M. (08/17/00). "ALARMING "YOU'S or DISARMING "I'S: POWER STRUGGLES vs. POWERFUL STRATEGIES PART I", http://www.selfhelpmagazine.com/articles/growth/aggression. html

Hankins, G. and Hankins, C. (1988). Prescription for Anger, New York:Warner.

Granath, J.; Ingvarsson, S.; and von Thiele, U. (2006). Stress management: A randomized study of cognitive behavior therapy and yoga. *Cognitive Behaviour Therapy*, 35(1), 3 – 10.

Heimberg, R.G., and Juster, H.R. (1994). Treatment of social phobia in cognitive behavioral groups. *Journal of Clinical Psychology*, 55, 38 – 46.

Hoyt, M.F. (1993). Group therapy in an HMO. *HMO Practice*, 7, 127 – 132.

Lerner, H.G. (2000). The Dance of Anger: A Woman's Guide to Changing the Patterns of Intimate Relationships, HarperTrade

Luhn, R. R. (1992) Managing Anger, Menlo Park, Cal.: Crisp Publications.

McKenzie, C. (05/28/98). "Anger what is it? and why – plus self test", http://www.performance-appraisals.org/cgi-bin/links/jump.cgi?ID=1702

Phillips, L.H.; Henry, J.D.; and Hosie, J.A. (2006). Age, anger regulation and well-being. *Aging & Mental Health*, 10(3), 250 – 256.

Potter-Efron, R. (2005). *Handbook of Anger Management: Individual, Couple, Family, and Group Approaches.* New York: Hawthorn Press, Inc.

Reilly, P.M., and Gruszski, R. (1984). A structured didactic model for men for controlling family violence. *International Journal of Offender Therapy and Comparative Criminology,* 28, 223 – 235.

Robertson, K. and Murachver, T. (2007). It takes two to tangles: Gender symmetry in intimate partner violence. *Basic and Applied Social Psychology,* 29(2), 109 –118.

Straus, M; Gelles, R.; and Steinmetz, S. (1980). *Behind Closed Doors: Voilence in the American Family.* Garden City, NY: Doubleday.

Tower, L.E. (2007). Group work with a new population: Women in domestic relationships responding to violence with violence. *Women and Therapy,* 30(1-2), 35 – 60.

Walker, L. (1979). *The Battered Woman.* New York: Harper & Row.

Yalom, I.D. (1995). *The Theory and Practice of Group Psychotherapy.* 4th ed. New York: Basic Books, Inc.

The Case of Anthony. Feindler, Eva L.; In: *Anger* related disorders: A practitioner's guide to comparative treatments. Feindler, Eva L.; New York, NY, US: Springer Publishing Co, 2006. pp. 29-42. [Chapter]

Review of Anger management: The complete treatment guidebook for practitioners. Smith, Kent; ANZJFT Australian and New Zealand Journal of Family Therapy, Vol 27(1), Mar 2006. pp. 56-57. [Review-Book]

Gender-specific symptoms of depression and anger attacks. Winkler, Dietmar; Pjrek, Edda; Kasper, Siegfried; Journal of Men's Health & Gender, Vol 3(1), Mar 2006. pp. 19-24. [Journal Article]

Review of Psychoanalysis, Violence and Rage-Type Murder. Asser, Jonathan; Psychodynamic Practice: Individuals, Groups and Organisations, Vol 12(1), Feb 2006. pp. 119-121. [Review-Book]

References for Groups

Charrier, G.O. (1974). Cog's ladder: A model of group development. In J.W. Pfeiffer & J.E. Jones (Eds.), The 1974 annual handbook for group facilitators. San Diego, CA: Pfeiffer & Company.

Cooke, P., & Widdis, W. (1988). Guidelines for interventions in groups. Unpublished manuscript.

Tuckman, B.W., & Jensen, M.A.C. (1977, December) Stages of small group development revisited. Group organization Studies, 2(4), 419427.

References For Emotional Intelligence

Antonakis, J. (2003). Why 'emotional intelligence' does not predict leadership effectiveness: A comment on Prati, Douglas, Ferris, Ameter, and Buckley. *The International Journal of Organizational Analysis, 11(4), 355-361.*

Antonakis, J. (2004). On why "emotional intelligence" will not predict leadership effectiveness beyond IQ or the "big five": An extension and rejoinder. Organizational Analysis, 12(2), 171-182.

Beasley, K. (1987, May) *The Emotional Quotient.* Mensa Magazine: United Kingdom Edition.

Bradberry, Travis. and Greaves, Jean. (2005). "The Emotional Intelligence Quickbook", New York: Simon and Schuster.

Bradberry, Travis and Greaves, Jean. "Hearless Bosses?" *Harvard Business Review*, December 1, 2005.

Bradberry, Travis. (2007). "The Personality Code," New York: Putnam

Ciarrochi, H. and Mayer, J. (2005). "Can Self-Report Measures Contribute to the Study of Emotional Intelligence? A Conversation between Joseph Ciarrochi and John D. Mayer" accessed January 2, 2006.

Darwin, C., 1872. Origin of Species, Sixth Edition. Senate, London.

Eysenck, H. (2000). *Intelligence: A New Look*, Transaction Publishers, (ISBN 0-7658-0707-6), pp. 109-110.

Fisher, Roger, and Shapiro, Daniel. (2005). *Beyond Reason: Using Emotions as You Negotiate. New York: Viking/Penguin.*

Freedman, J. (2007). *At the heart of leadership*. California: Six Seconds.

Gardner, H. (1975) *The Shattered Mind*. New York: Knopf.

Gibbs, Nancy (1995, October 2). The EQ Factor. *Time Magazine*. Web reference at http://www.time.com/time/classroom/psych/unit5_article1. html accessed January 2, 2006.

Goleman, D. (1996). *Emotional Intelligence: why it can matter more than IQ*. London : Bloomsbury. (ISBN 0-7475-2622-2) MacCann, C., Roberts, R.D., Matthews, G., & Zeidner, M. (2004). Consensus scoring and empirical option weighting of performance-based emotional intelligence tests. *Personality & Individual Differences, 36*, 645-662.

Mayer, J. (2005a). "Can Emotional Knowledge be Improved? Can you raise emotional intelligence?" The University of New Hampshire. Web reference at http://www.unh.edu/emotional_intelligence/ei%20 Improve/ei%20Rasing%20EI.htmaccessed January 2, 2006.

Mayer, J. (2005b) "Emotional Intelligence Information: A Site Dedicated to Communicating Scientific Information about Emotional Intelligence, Including Relevant Aspects of Emotions, Cognition, and Personality."

The University of New Hampshire. Web reference at http://www.unh. edu/emotional_intelligence/index.html accessed January 2, 2006.

Mayer, J. (2005c). "Is EI the Best Predictor of Success in Life?" The University of New Hampshire. Web reference at http://www.unh. edu/emotional_intelligence/ei%20Controversies/eicontroversy1%20 best%20predictor.htm accessed January 2, 2006.

Mayer, J. (2005c). "How Do You Measure Emotional Intelligence?" The University of New Hampshire. Web reference at [1] accessed January 2, 2006.

Mayer, J.D. & Salovey, P. (1993). The intelligence of emotional intelligence. *Intelligence*, 17, 433-442.

Mayer, J., Salovey, P., Caruso, D.R., and Sitarenios, G. (2001) "Emotional intelligence as a standard intelligence." *Emotion*, 1, 232-242.

Payne, W.L. (1985). A study of emotion: developing emotional intelligence; self-integration; relating to fear, pain and desire (theory, structure of reality, problem-solving, contraction/expansion, tuning in/ coming out/letting go). A Doctoral Dissertation. Cincinnati, OH: The Union For Experimenting Colleges And Universities (now The Union Institute). Abstract available at http://eqi.org/payne.htm

Roberts, R.D., Zeidner, M., and Matthews, G. (2001). Does emotional intelligence meet traditional standards for an intelligence? Some new data and conclusions. *Emotion, 1*, p. 196-231. Web pre-publication version available at http://eqi.org/ei_abs4.htm accessed 19 Sept 2006.

Salovey, P. & David S. (Ed.s). (1997). Emotional development and Emotional Intelligence: Educational implications. New York: Basic Books. (ISBN 978-0465095872)

Salovey, P. and Mayer, J.D. (1990). "Emotional intelligence." *Imagination, Cognition, and Personality*, 9(1990), 185-211. [2]

Schutte, N.S., Malouff, J.M., Hall, L.E., Haggerty, D.J., Cooper, J.T., Golden, C.J., & Dornheim, L. (1998). Development and validation of a measure of emotional intelligence. Personality and Individual Differences, 25, 167-177.

Smith, M. K. (2002) "Howard Gardner and multiple intelligences," *the encyclopedia of informal education*, Downloaded from http://www.infed. org/thinkers/gardner.htm on October 31, 2005.

Stein, S and Book, H. "The EQ Edge". Toronto: Jossey-Bass.

Stein, S (1997). Men and Women Have Different Kinds and Levels of Emotional Intelligence, EQ for Both Sexes is Key to Workplace Success.

Technical Brochures regarding the psychometric properties of the BOEI (Benchmark of Emotional Intelligence), EQ-i, and MSCEIT.

Tett, R. P., Fox, K. E., & Wang, A. (2005). Development and validation of a self-report measure of emotional intelligence as a multidimensional trait domain. *Personality and Social Psychology Bulletin, 31,* 859-888.

Thorndike, R.K. (1920). "Intelligence and Its Uses," *Harper's Magazine* 140, 227-335.

Warneka, T. (2006). *Leading People the Black Belt Way: Conquering the Five Core Problems Facing Leaders Today.* Asogomi Press. Cleveland, Ohio.

Waterhouse, Lynn. (2006a). Multiple Intelligences, the Mozart Effect, and Emotional Intelligence: A critical review. Educational Psychologist, 41(4), Fall, pp. 207-225.

Waterhouse, Lynn. (2006b). "Inadequate Evidence for Multiple Intelligences, Mozart Effect, and Emotional Intelligence Theories." Educational Psychologist, 41(4), Fall, pp. 247-255.

Printed in the United States
By Bookmasters